D0114754

Josh McDowell —

I can honestly say that I am more resolved to disciple my own children as a result of
...having the privilege of reading *Let Us Highly Resolve*. This resource is so critical,
and strategic in raising families that will stand for Christ and that's what every dad
and every mom wants. *Let Us Highly Resolve* is a powerful resource."

Mary Pride —

Let Us Highly Resolve is a life-changing book.

Cathy Duffy —

"In *Let Us Highly Resolve*, the Quines give us a 'handbook' for raising our children
according to [the Biblical] world view. From building upon the biblical foundation
and teaching our children absolutes and proper reasoning, we can build our families
up in faith, truth, and knowledge, equipping them to carry the message of the gospel
to the world. The Quines show us how we can raise our children to "challenge our
culture with the truth of Christianity." You might consider this sort of a foundational
book on the philosophy of raising families and of education. Some of the ideas are
very profound and challenging, but the Quines translate those ideas into real life with
many stories from their own lives and experiences. If you are interested in doing
more than just "getting through school" with your children, *this is a must read*."

Diana Waring —

"*Let Us Highly Resolve* deals with one of the most important issues facing us as
Christian parents today — raising our children in a Biblical world view. That is the
core, the very foundation, of who we are and why we do what we do, especially as it
concerns our parenting. David and Shirley have issued a clarion call to us all, the call
to carefully, thoughtfully, and Biblically prepare our children to be leaders in the
21st century. I encourage you to read this book prayerfully. It may be the most important book you ever read!"

Carole Seid, *Barnabas Books*

"Teaching Christians to think "Christianly " is the most important task we will ever
accomplish. *Let Us Highly Resolve* is my heart in print."

Bob and Tina Farewell, *Lifetime Books*

"Being friends, as well as guests in David and Shirley Quine's home, has been a major highlight for our family. We are always blessed by observing first hand the Quine's philosophy of life in action. For those who are not able to be edified by their physical hospitality, you are sure to be inspired by their book, *Let Us Highly Resolve*."

Jay Marshall, Senior Pastor, Southern California

"*Let Us Highly Resolve* is a great work that will provide significant help to Christians in fighting the battle in our culture. David has a unique gift for weaving the interpretations of history with the Word of God. Deep insight is gained and the Word of God comes alive as he shows how it counters the philosophies of men."

Susan Thurlow, author

"This is a significant work. It clarifies vital cultural issues we face as Christian families entering the 21st century. The book helps to sharpen our focus, better preparing Christians for the cultural challenges we will face in the future. I was personally challenged enough [after reading *Let Us Highly Resolve*] to make significant changes in our school curriculum. Mark and I feel that preparing our children to reason from a biblical perspective, to discern what the world's perspective is and to let the light of Christ in them impact their own area of influence, is a priority in their education."

Israel Wayne, *Home School Digest*

"There is a tremendous need, in our present time, for parents to actively and systematically equip their children with a clear, definitive Biblical world view. David and Shirley's book is a wake-up call to complacent Christian living in a militant, secular world."

Dale Simpson, *Homeschooling Today*

"*Let Us Highly Resolve* encourages and challenges me to help my children see the flow of human thought across history. My children need the big picture and this book helps them get it."

Let Us Highly Resolve

Preparing Families to Enter the 21st Century

DAVID AND SHIRLEY QUINE

Cornerstone Curriculum
Richardson, Texas 75080

Front Cover:
Jean-Honoré Fragonard (French, 1732-1806)
The Visit to the Nursery, before 1784, oil on canvas
Courtesy of National Gallery of Art, Washington, D.C.
Samuel H. Kress Collection

This tender scene is of a young girl who set aside wealth and position for life in the countryside with a poor but virtuous man. Bending over the cradle the two lovingly look at the child — holding hands and smiling, cherishing this precious moment. Grandmother and children are blessed by the love displayed. The focus of Fragonard is on family life and domestic virtue.

"Lord, bless my own home, and give me grace as one of Your redeemed ones, to train my children for their God. May the joy of a personal experience of redemption and the love of the blessed Redeemer, warm my heart, inspire my words, and light up my life to testify of You and train them for You alone. Amen."
Raising Your Children For Christ by Andrew Murray

Let Us Highly Resolve copyright © 1996 by David and Shirley Quine
All rights reserved. Written permission must be secured from the publisher to use or reproduce any part of this book, except for quotations in reviews or articles.

Third Printing
Printed in the United States of America
Library of Congress Catalog Card Number: 96-93112
ISBN 0-9656512-0-7

Pictured on the back cover:
David and Shirley Quine with their children:
Betsy, Byron, Bryce
Brett, Ben, Blaine, Bonney
Blessing, Bethany

Published by
THE CORNERSTONE CURRICULUM PROJECT
2006 FLAT CREEK PLACE
RICHARDSON, TEXAS 75080
972-235-5149

To the Christian parents of our day and generation, to the sons and daughters of whom we are the mothers and the fathers, and to the children that our children will be raising

LET US HIGHLY RESOLVE

To prepare our families to enter the twenty-first century to the glory of God.

Contents

THOUGHTS FROM OUR CHILDREN 9

Preface 11

Resolve Number One
TO BUILD OUR FAMILIES UPON THE BIBLICAL WORLD VIEW 17

Resolve Number Two
TO ESTABLISH OUR CHILDREN'S LIVES UPON TRUTH AND ABSOLUTES . 33

Resolve Number Three
TO EQUIP OUR CHILDREN TO REASON 45

Resolve Number Four
TO ENTER INTO TRUE SPIRITUALITY 65

Resolve Number Five
TO BE "BY FAITH" FAMILIES 79

Resolve Number Six
TO PREPARE OUR CHILDREN
AS A 'LETTER OF CHRIST' TO THE CULTURE 89

Resolve Number Seven
TO CHALLENGE OUR CULTURE WITH THE TRUTH OF CHRISTIANITY
AND THE LIFE OF CHRIST 103

Postscript 121

Thoughts from our Children

Ideas have consequences. This is true whether one is referring to philosophy, theology, music, art, or law. A person's outlook on the world will shape his actions. During the last 120 years this nation has departed significantly from the thinking of our Founding Fathers. This is why I have decided to dedicate my life to working in the governmental system to bring back the world view of those men who founded our country.

It has always been my parents' goal to prepare and equip me for whatever career I would ultimately choose. Throughout my childhood school was not just formal education. Every day my father and I would discuss the events in the world and examine the world views of the leaders, past and present. This teaching dealt with much more than facts, it was concerned with ideas. This kind of education has prepared me to look beyond the individual laws or specific court decisions and to look for the ideas that are behind the actions of world leaders. Without this kind of training I would be lost in a sea of confusion.

— Bryce, 21 years old

Music is one of God's wonderful gifts to man. Through it we may praise our heavenly Father, express vast emotion, or communicate ideas with extraordinary power. I am grateful that I was introduced at an early age to classical music. Music is as an integral part of our family life.

I am currently studying as a pianist. I want to offer to my heavenly Father music that will bring glory to Him while revealing something of his nature and character to our culture.

Classical music can reflect God's character through its order, structure, continuity, and beauty. This relationship is essential. Just as God's character is the standard for our lives, it must be the basis for music as well. Christians have the unique ability to create music because we have a personal relationship with the Author of all beauty. Our lives should be a song of praise to God.

— Ben, 19 years old

"You're absolutely right!" he said. But is it really possible to be absolutely right? Most people in mainstream society would answer emphatically, "Absolutely not!" Ironically that is the way many people have been taught to think and act. "There are no rules" or if there are rules, then they are set by the individual at that specific place, or time and can be terminated or modified whenever they cease to give what adequate freedom they were supposed to give - since it is incorrectly thought that freedom is only found in either no rules or your own set of personal rules.

I have been blessed to grow up in a family that believes in absolutes without exception. The value of such a belief, and the knowledge of how it should be applied is inestimable. Without it a person becomes like a ship without an anchor that drifts along in the sea ever tossed about on the waves of volatile thoughts and emotions — ever changing, never lasting, in that world of ultimate freedom, and ultimate enslavement to meaninglessness.

As one friend of mine said regarding language: "You know why I like slangs (words without an absolute meaning). It's because they're so useful! They can mean anything you want them to mean!" I explained, "The only problem is however, that if a word has all meaning relatively, can't it be argued that it has no meaning absolutely and therefore no true communication can occur?" While absolutes in language may seem unimportant, the same principles hold true for them as for important matters like ethics and morality. Therefore, if you want a foundation on which to build, if you want something that will be true today and tomorrow, you absolutely must find the Absolutes.

— Blaine, 16 years old

Everyone has a world view whether they realize it or not. Ideas are the motivation for decisions made throughout life. Our society offers many opportunities for making bad choices. How we spend our time, the people we choose to be our friends, and the music we listen to are only a few choices which are affected by our world view. For us to be adequately prepared to make right choices we must hold beliefs which are based upon absolute truth. Only as we build our lives upon the Biblical world view we will have a real basis for knowing right and wrong in our personal lives.

— Betsy, 16 years old
— Blessing, 13 years old

LET US HIGHLY RESOLVE

But Daniel resolved not to defile himself.

— Daniel 1:8

For I resolved to know nothing while I was with you except Jesus Christ and him crucified.

— 1 Corinthians 2:2

And it came about when the days were approaching for his ascension that he resolutely set his face to go to Jerusalem.

— Luke 9:51

To Resolve

Determined in purpose ...
To follow some course of action ...
A resolution or determination made ...
With steady perseverance - firmly determined ...
To fix or settle on by a deliberate choice and will ...
Constant in pursuing a purpose... Having a fixed purpose
Steadfast; bold; firm determination, steady, unshaken firmness

youth of royal or noble birth was taken into captivity by a conquering country. This young Hebrew man named Daniel showed great promise physically, intellectually, and socially. A select group of youth were being prepared for personal service to their new king. Daniel was to be taught by the finest teachers. The objective was to replace the thoughts and ideas that he had grown up with as Truth with a complete set of new ideas. His heart and mind were to be conformed to the thoughts and ideas, to the laws and customs of this new country. In addition, this change in culture included a change in food. The most dramatic attempt to replace this young man's world view came when his name was changed from 'God is Judge' to 'May Bel protect his life' (Daniel 1:7).

This education was to be an intense three-year indoctrination for the purpose of conforming Daniel to the culture and thinking of Babylon. The truth that he had been taught from childhood was to be replaced with a different way of looking at life — a different world view. He had been caught in the cross fire of two very different cultures — two very different world views. How would he respond?

We read "But Daniel resolved not to defile himself...."(Daniel 1:8). Though his surroundings, his food, and his name were all changed, Daniel, by a deliberate choice of his will, determined to remain firm in his convictions. He *resolved* to suffer unknown consequences rather than change his heart and mind to these new ideas.

Our word *resolve* comes from the roots *re* + *solvere*, which means to *loosen* or *untie*. While it is easy to become entangled in the ideas, the thoughts, and customs of a culture, Daniel determined not to be tied to the world view of the Babylonian culture. He resolved to firmly fix his life upon the true and living God.

In the 18th Chapter of the Book of Acts we find the apostle Paul arriving in Corinth after a very difficult experience in Athens. Because the philosophers in Athens had sneered at the message of the resurrection, was Paul tempted to incorporate some of the thoughts and ideas of the Greek philosophers into what he would say to those in Corinth? Would not the Good News of Jesus Christ be more acceptable to the Corinthians if he slightly modified his message?

Yet we read that Paul firmly purposed and determined — he *resolved* — "to know nothing among [them] except Jesus Christ, and Him crucified" (I Corinthians 2:2). He resolved not to rely upon his own strength, his own knowledge, or his own ability to communicate the truth of Christ to those in Corinth. Choosing not to rely upon the wisdom of man, Paul *resolved* to rest upon the power and revelation of God. Did that mean he was not going to use reason and evidence to support the claims of Christ? Certainly not. However, Paul wanted all to know that the wisdom, the knowledge, and the power of which he was speaking were of God, not of man! The sole source and authority of Paul's message was Divine Revelation — "to the Jews a stumbling block, and to Gentiles foolishness..." (I Corinthians 1:23).

Jesus knew that the time for fulfilling His purpose was quickly approaching. Knowing that He would not be coming as the King, but rather as the sacrifice, He 'resolutely set his face to go to Jerusalem' (Luke 9:51). He would not be distracted by his humanness. He set aside all earthly feelings and firmly determined and purposed to focus upon the ascension knowing full well that the way of His ascension involved His own personal humiliation and crucifixion. Jesus had firmly established in His mind the course pre-planned by the Trinity before the creation of the world, the salvation of mankind.

The end of the 20th century is filled with a multitude of thoughts and ideas which are contrary to the Christian world view and which are seeking to distract us. Christian families must not be tied to the false ideas of this century and culture. Rather, we must, like Daniel, Paul, and Jesus, resolve to untie ourselves from the false notions that seek to entangle us and hold our minds tied captive. By fixing our thoughts on truth, we can chart a path, set a course of action, for both ourselves and our children as we enter into the 21st century.

THEREFORE, LET US HIGHLY RESOLVE …

To build our families upon the Biblical world view.
To establish our children's lives upon truth and absolutes.
To equip our children to reason.
To enter into true spirituality.
To be 'by faith' families.
To prepare our children as a 'Letter of Christ' to the culture.
To challenge our culture with the truth of Christianity and life of Christ.

Samuel Adams, architect of the War for Independence and cousin of John Adams the second President of the United States, said in 1771, "Let us contemplate our forefathers and posterity and *resolve* to maintain the rights bequeathed to us from the former, for the sake of the latter. The necessity of the times, more than ever, calls for our utmost circumspection, deliberation, fortitude, and perseverance. Let us remember that 'if we suffer tamely a lawless attack upon our liberty, we encourage it, and involve others in our doom.' It is a very serious consideration that millions yet unborn may be the miserable sharers of the event."[1] *Circumspection* means to be careful to consider all circumstances and possible consequences. *Deliberation* means to consider the reasons for and against a measure. *Fortitude* is the strength of mind that enables a person to encounter danger or bear pain or adversity with courage. *Perseverance* means to persist in an undertaking in spite of counter influences, opposition, or discouragement. We who stand at the doorway to the 21st century must adopt this same resolve. As the Founding Fathers, we too are living in difficult times. Because we do not want to be foolhardy, we must deliberately resolve to base our lives upon the Biblical world view.

However, even as we make these resolves, there may arise doubts and fears. These two reactions paralyze our confidence in God. Today, we find ourselves in much the same situation as Joshua. Moses had died. Joshua was to lead the people of Israel against the 'giants' of the land. What did God say to him? We read in Joshua chapter 1 verses 6 and 7 "Be strong and courageous … Only be strong and very courageous.…" Turn back to the book of Deuteronomy (chapter 31 verses 6-8):

> Be strong and courageous, do not be afraid or tremble at them, for the Lord your God is the one who goes with you.

He will not fail you or forsake you." Then Moses called to Joshua and said to him in the sight of all Israel, "Be strong and courageous, for you shall go with this people into the land which the Lord has sworn to their fathers to give them, and you shall give it to them as an inheritance. And the Lord is the one who goes ahead of you; He will be with you. He will not fail you or forsake you. Do no fear, or be dismayed."

Joshua was to take courage knowing that (1) God was with him; (2) God would not fail him; (3) God would not forsake (leave) him; (4) God was giving him the promise made to Abraham; and, (5) God would go ahead of him.

Based upon the fact that these things were absolute truth, Joshua was not to fear or to be dismayed! Although we are not conquering geographical areas like Joshua, we are in a raging battle. The Apostle Paul says that, "We are destroying speculations and every lofty thing raised up against the knowledge of God and we are taking every thought captive to the obedience of Christ" (II Corinthians 10:5). It is imperative that we underscore the point that Paul did not say we are to destroy people who hold different beliefs!

We must become skilled at destroying the false notions that people are basing their lives upon without destroying the people. If we do not destroy these false ideas, then these false ideas will certainly destroy the people!

You might be thinking, "Are the promises made to Joshua also true for us? We know how God worked in the lives of people in the Old Testament, but what about us today?" We must know what the New Testament says about God's involvement in our lives as He sends us into battle.

God is with us (John 14; I Corinthians 3:16).

God will not fail us (Romans 8:31-39; I Corinthians. 15:57).

God will not desert us (Luke 15: 11-32; Romans 8: 32-39; restated in Hebrews 13:5).

God will not forsake us (Ephesians 1:5, 14).

It is imperative that our resolve be based upon absolute truth. It is then, and only then, that we can have the confidence and courage needed to enter into the battle for the people of the 21st century.

The single most important topic as we prepare and equip our children to enter the 21st century is an understanding of world views. A person's world view is the basis for the personal decisions he makes, and it becomes the arbitrator by which he evaluates the thoughts and ideas that surround him. Francis Schaeffer explains that, "Most people catch their [world view] from their family and surrounding society the way a child catches measles. But people with more understanding realize that their presuppositions should be chosen after a careful consideration of what world view is true."[2]

Teaching our children from the Christian world view perspective must be a conscious decision. This preparation is too important to leave to chance. *TIME*[3] magazine predicts that the citizens of the 21st century will have no knowledge, no interest, and no need of our God. Others are saying that school children of today will view the God of the Bible as we view the gods of Greece and Rome and that school children of the 21st century will be taught 'Christian Mythology.' If our children are going to be able to stand against the thoughts and ideas of the 21st Century and be able to defend their faith, we must be teaching, equipping, and preparing them now. Nothing is of greater importance. All of life should be understood from the Christian world view.

The Psalmist asks: *When the foundations are destroyed, what are the righteous to do* (Psalm 11:3)? We must be reestablishing our lives and the lives of our family upon the Biblical world view. There is no greater work in which to be called. Gene Stratton-Porter, writing to her generation, expresses our convictions:

> When I think of the life that we are leading, of the uses to which we have put the bounty provided for us by the Almighty, when I think of the greed and the lust and the selfishness that is crowding everything that is high and holy and delicate, that is kind and loving and considerate of our fellow men, from our hearts, I wish that I might attain to some high peak from which my voice could reach to the ends of the earth, and that there I might cry out to the men and women of my day and generation, to the men and women of whom we are the mothers and the fathers, and to the children that our children are rearing, I wish that I might cry out:
> L E T   U S   H I G H L Y   R E S O L V E
> that we will do everything that our day and location permits actually to put into practice the teachings of Jesus Christ.[4]

Resolve Number One

TO BUILD OUR FAMILIES UPON THE BIBLICAL WORLD VIEW

We are no longer to be children, tossed here and there by waves, and carried about by every wind of doctrine, by the trickery of men, by craftiness in deceitful scheming; but speaking the truth in love.
— Ephesians. 4:14,15

There is a flow to history and culture. This flow is rooted and has its wellspring in the thoughts of people....Most people catch their [world view] from their family and surrounding society the way a child catches measles. But people with more understanding realize that their presuppositions should be chosen after a careful consideration of what world view is true. [1]
— Dr. Francis Schaeffer

The Biblical world view is the gauge against which we measure our ideas and our lives. Our goal is a valid world-life view. [2]
— Gladys Hunt

We have to think in new ways! [3]
— Hillary Rodham Clinton

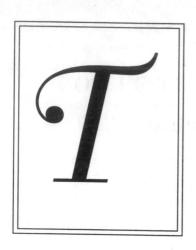

There is no single topic of greater importance as we prepare our children to enter into the 21st century than world views. In a *Parade* magazine (April 1993) interview Hillary Rodham Clinton explains that "We have to think in new ways!"[4] Three questions come to mind as one considers this decision: (1) How are the old ways of thinking different from the new ways? (2) Which way of thinking is based upon truth and absolutes and which is based upon relativism? and, (3) What happens to a person or people that embrace either the new or old way of thinking? A way of thinking is a world view. Francis Schaeffer explains that we must help our children choose "after a careful consideration of what world view is true." [5]

Building a World View

To help explain what is meant by *world view* may we suggest a simple activity. In your mind or on a sheet of paper, draw the outline of the continental United States. Next, picture the state of your birth in its proper position and proportion. Sketch several states around your birth state. How have you done so far? Next, put the point of your pencil where you think the Mississippi River begins. Meander it down the page to where you think it empties into the

Gulf of Mexico. If you were born east of the Mississippi River, sketch several states on the west side. If you were born west of the Mississippi River, then draw three or four of the states on the east side — several of the easier states like Rhode Island, Vermont or Delaware.

Several years ago I asked our children to do this activity. Blessing, who was about six at the time, was only asked to draw the outline of the State of Texas. Roughly, it looked like a shovel. However, at the top there were two circles. I was a little puzzled. I asked her to tell me about the two circles. She looked up at me and said, "Daddy, those are the 'Eyes of Texas.'"

How does your map look? If it looks like mine, the further we move from our home state the more indistinct and distorted our map becomes. Keep in mind this is our picture — our view — of the United States or at least how we are able to articulate our view.

James Sire explains that a world view is "a map of reality. And like any map it may fit what is really there or it may be grossly misleading."[6] A world view is a picture or perspective of life. There is a certain place in our thinking that we feel at home. The further individuals, or culture move away from this home base the more fuzzy our thinking becomes. It is then that we begin to feel uncomfortable and become inconsistent in our behavior. Because we all have poor maps, God is in the process of correcting our map of life. He has given us the Scriptures, His Son and Spirit, and certain God-ordained circumstances to correct our picture of who He is and what He is doing in our lives. God has also used music, art, science, and literature to redraw our image of Himself.

Correcting My Map

"Daddy, can we pray for a baby brother?"
"Not tonight, son," was my response.
"But you wouldn't last night either."
"I know. Maybe, tomorrow night."
"But I want a little baby brother!"

That was a conversation I was having with our third son for more than six months. We already had five children. Their ages were eight, six, twins that were four, and a one-year-old. Shirley was teaching our children at home, which was very demanding, while I was working several jobs. We were living in a small three bedroom house in a suburb of Dallas, Texas. Having come from a small family myself, I was exhausted and felt that there was 'no room in the inn' with no vacancy in the near future.

I thought to myself: *How could God be so inconsiderate as to make us live in such close quarters? Had He not said that He would meet all our needs? Didn't that include housing? If God wanted us to have more children, then first He would have to provide more space! Besides weren't we out of step with culture as it was? We had something like 2.75 times the national average! Even those within the Church wondered if we knew the basic 'facts of life.'*

Shirley and I had heard many times that only two things will go into eternity: God's Word and people. But for us to have more children seemed like going just a little bit too far. I had reached a barrier in my life.

During World War II, airplanes had approached but not broken the sound barrier. Many had tried, but all were turned back. It was not until October 14, 1947 that General Chuck Yeager was able to break the sound barrier in the X-1 rocket research plane. This new breakthrough propelled the aerospace industry to new heights.

Though I was not at the sound barrier, I found myself at the faith barrier. Would I go on or be turned back? I could not envision how we could possibly make enough money to support more children. We were just barely making it as it was. I also wondered where we would put more children if we had more. *God would have to change my circumstances first. Then I would consider whether to trust Him in this area* was my attitude. My map was distorted. I was attempting to maneuver and manipulate God.

It was at this same time that we were reading *Heidi* aloud to our children. The book gave me a peek into her life situation which gave me Godly insight about our circumstances and my map:

> "Ah, Heidi, that brings light to the heart! What a comfort you have brought me!" And the old woman kept on repeating the glad words, while Heidi beamed with happiness, and she could not take her eyes away from the grandmother's face, which had never looked like that before. She had no longer the old troubled expression, but was alight with peace and joy as if she were already looking with clear new eyes into the garden of Paradise ... Heidi shouted for joy at the thought that grandmother would never need any more to eat hard black bread, and "Oh, grandfather!" she said, "everything is happier now than it has ever been in our lives before!" and she

sang and skipped along, holding her grandfather's hand as lighthearted as a bird. But all at once she grew quiet and said, "If God had let me come at once, as I prayed, then everything would have been different, I should only have had a little bread to bring to grandmother, and I should not have been able to read, which is such a comfort to her; but God has arranged it all so much better than I knew how to; everything has happened just as the other grandmother said it would. Oh, how glad I am that God did not let me have at once all I prayed and wept for! And now I shall always pray to God as she told me, and always thank Him, and when He does not do anything I ask for I shall think to myself, It's just like it was in Frankfurt: God, I am sure, is going to do something better still."[7]

Since God knows all possible combinations of outcomes and all consequences of all possible decisions, and since nothing is allowed to touch our lives that He does not first pass through His hands, then He can be trusted for the moment-by-moment circumstances in our daily lives.

How thankful I am that He did not give to us a larger house at once as we prayed. How often I look back to this sign post in my life and think to myself, "It's just like it was in that time in my life: God, I am sure, is going to arrange it all so much better than I know how to. God is going to do something far better still." God has used stories like these to help correct and to redraw my map, my picture of life. They help me gain perspective — God's perfect perspective on what He is trying to do in my own life. In our dinning room we recently placed the MANUSCRIPTURE: *For I know the plans I have for you, declares the Lord, plans to prosper you and not to harm you, plans to give you hope and a future* (Jeremiah 29:11).

After Blaine's persistence of more than six months, I finally agreed that if he would pray I would listen. God was making some headway with me. It was not long afterwards that I too joined in and began praying with him. About nine months later our fourth son, Byron, was born. God had answered Blaine's prayer. It was a double miracle. He had answered Blaine's prayer and He had changed my life. I was learning to 'look not at the things which are seen, but at the things which are not seen' — not in our temporal home and circumstances in which we were living but in the eternal value of our children.

However, God did not stop there. Since that time, He has given us Bethany, Bonney, and most recently Brett. Can you believe it? We now have nine children and until just recently we lived in the same three-bedroom house. I found the idea expressed by Rees Howells regarding those to whom he was ministering had become my heart attitude: "After many hard experiences we found the resting place. We became like waiters serving in a restaurant; it wasn't our business whether ten, fifteen or twenty would come, we knew the Manager would not fail to provide what was needed. We told the Lord to send as many as He liked!"[8] By refocusing my attention, God was teaching me to walk by faith at a totally new level. I had broken the faith barrier.

Our Heavenly Father is concerned about what we go through. However, He is more concerned with how we respond to what we go through. That part of my map was being redrawn. He allows circumstances to come into our lives so that we have the opportunity to respond either by the way we feel or by faith.

Has God been faithful? He has been abundantly more faithful than we could ever have thought or asked. Are we being irresponsible, illogical, or irrational in the choices we are making? From the twentieth century perspective, the answer is 'yes'; however, from an eternal perspective, an emphatic 'no' is the answer.

Multiple Maps

Because a map is a representation of what is real, it serves as a guide to direct a person in his travels. *Where am I? Where am I going? and How will I get there?* These are vital questions we answer as we look at a map. The ability to get to our final destination is determined by the accuracy of the map, and our ability and willingness to follow its directions.

We were on our way to Amarillo, Texas from Oklahoma City. I was a very young child at the time. My dad asked, "Where do we turn?" It sounds strange to our ears today, but I remember my mom saying, "The road map says to go about two miles past the large oak tree and turn right on the first road past the large white house." I also remember that we got lost quite often. Maps have certainly changed over time.

Since a world view is like a map, the ability to navigate through life is dependent not only upon the accuracy and detail of the map, but also upon how well we are able and willing to follow it. World views provide answers to life's basic questions: *Who am I? Where am I from?* and *Where am I going?* The first question focuses our thoughts on the nature of man, the second with our origin, and the last with our destiny. These are the important questions we answer as we navigate through life. What are the basic answers to these questions? Although there can only be one true map of reality, in the history of Western culture there have been two major competing world views: two maps, two sets of ideas. You can think of it like this: there is the true map and there also exists a counterfeit map. In order for our families to navigate through life, it is imperative that we are able to 'read' the various maps in order to determine which map truly represents reality. For example, regarding the rearing of children, which view most closely reflects reality? One view says that children are to be raised by a mother and father. The other view says , "It takes a village to raise a child."[9] The former view reflects the idea of the Biblical world view. The latter view was proposed by Plato in antiquity and most recently by President Bill Clinton during the 1996 reelection campaign.

Which set of answers is most consistent with the world as we know it? The way a child or culture answers these and other similar questions will dramatically influence the present and future. We must, as Dr. Schaeffer has exhorted us, help our children to choose *after a careful consideration of which world view is true.*

During certain times of history, one world view overshadows the others. In other times the various world views battle for the control of the hearts and minds of the people. The two dominant perspectives in Western culture in this century are the Biblical world view and the secular world view. The New Age, a third view, appears to be a rising star with great potential for persuading people to accept its position. Perhaps the challenge from this view will succeed in toppling one or both of the other two views and become the predominant world view of the west. In an attempt to attract followers, the New Age is a blend of Eastern religions and Western naturalism. As the culture moves further from Christianity and as those in the culture recognize that secularism offers no spiritual dimension of life, the New Age, with its blending of the 'spiritual' with the natural may well become the dominant world view. How does each world view answer the basic questions of life? How are they alike or different?

Who Am I? Where Am I From? and Where Am I Going?

The Biblical World View

From the Biblical world view, man is both like other created life and yet at the same time significantly different. Because God is infinite and the rest of His creation including man are finite, man finds himself more like the plants and animals. On the other hand, because man is created in the image of God (Genesis 1:26), he is set apart from the rest of the creation. To be in the "image of something" is to take on its characteristics. On a coin, the image of the person and letters are impressed into the silver or gold. The coin takes on the image of the imprint. Somewhat like a coin, man is impressed with the image of God. Man, unlike the plant or animal kingdoms, is able to make moral choices. He is able to worship, to reason, and to express his creativity.

Man was originally created good. He was set in a perfect environment with a perfect Father (Genesis 1 and 2). He was created to live in harmony with God, his wife and family, his environment, and with himself. However, since he is not a robot, pre-programmed to make certain choices, he is able to decide for himself the moral decisions he will make and the direction he will take (Genesis 2: 16, 17). Even in the best environment man decided to question the authority and integrity of God and willfully chose to disobey Him (Genesis 3: 1-20). The consequences for this choice affected not only Adam and Eve, but each generation to follow. In addition, the rest of creation was set on a course of destruction. As a result, the world in which we live is now abnormal; that is to say, it is not as it was originally intended to be (Genesis 3: 17-24). The ability to know and choose right from wrong has become confused; man can no longer reason consistently and coherently; and his creativity has become blurred from reality. This is the nature, the characteristic, of man today.

However, God chose to enter into history for the purpose of restoring His creation to its original condition. Through the work of Jesus Christ, God has made available to man the opportunity to be "transformed by the renewing of our minds" (Romans 12:2). This process begins at new birth, followed by growing to spiritual maturity. This will not be complete, however, until His return. At that time in addition to man being restored, the creation itself will be put back together (Romans 8:18-22). Although Humpty-Dumpty was unable to be pieced back together, we look forward to a time in which God will take this abnormal world and restore it to its original position.

What happens to man at death? is the final question. Does he simply cease to exist, or does he continue to live? If he does continue living, does he return in a different form, or is he moved into a different realm? The Biblical world view is quite clear regarding this point. Man, at death, either enters into the presence of God forever, or he is set in a state forever separated from God. Of course, man's choice regarding Christ and His work on the cross determines the answer to this final question. The Biblical world view gives good, sufficient, and adequate answers to man's basic questions.

The Secular World View

Hillary Clinton, in an interview with *Parade Magazine*, said that, "We have to think in new ways."[10] What is the basis of this *new way of thinking*?

To find the answer to this question, we must go deeper into her interview. She was asked who the most influential people were in the development of her thinking.[11] These people included Albert Camus, e e cummings, and Pablo Picasso. Who were these three people? What ideas did they have about life? Should we begin to think like them?

Albert Camus, an existential novelist and playwright, received the Nobel Prize for Literature in 1957. *The World Book Encyclopedia* describes Camus in the following way:

> He argued that people hang on to life even though life has no meaning or purpose to justify it and is thus absurd.... Camus was concerned with the freedom and responsibility of the individual, the alienation of the individual from society, and the difficulty of facing life without the comfort of believing in God or in absolute moral standards.[12]

This view of life would certainly represent a *new way of thinking*, opposing the traditional Judeo-Christian heritage of Western culture. For more than 19 centuries, Western civilization rested upon the belief in God and absolute moral standards. Alexis de Toqueville, describing American life during the 1830's, said:

> I sought for the key to the greatness and genius of America in her harbors... in her fertile fields and boundless forests; in her rich mines and vast world commerce; in her public school system and institutions of learning. I sought for it in her democratic Congress and in her matchless Constitution.
> Not until I went into the churches of America and heard her pulpits flame with righteousness did I understand the secret of her genius and power.
> America is great because America is good, and if America ever ceases to be good, America will cease to be great.[13]

America's goodness rested upon it's belief in the infinite-personal God!

What about e e cummings? (No, this is not a typographical error. This 20th century America author wrote his name: lower case 'e', lower case 'e', lower case 'c', cummings.) The 1953 edition of *The World Book Encyclopedia* correlates grammar and arithmetic rules:

> When we add or subtract, divide or multiply, we do so according to rules. If we do not, we get the wrong answer. In the same way, when we speak or write, we ought to do so according to rules. If we do not use the rules, other people may not understand what we say.[14]

Not so according to e e cummings! He introduced a *new way of communicating*. He had a total disregard for rules of grammar and punctuation. He made up his own words, ran words together, and abandoned the use of capital letters. tohimruleswerebinding. cummings' ideas are reminiscent of the ideas of Rousseau. He thought and taught that the order, structure, and boundaries of European Christianity during the 1700's were keeping society from reaching its true greatness. Maybe this *new way of thinking* is not so new after all?

I was enrolled in freshman composition at college during the Vietnam War era. If your grades were good enough, then you had an exempt status. At the university I attended, freshman composition was the class which determined whether you stayed in college or were sent to Southeast Asia. The first day of class the professor said we would write a composition during each class. However, because there were no rules of grammar or punctuation, there was no need to worry. Whew! That was a relief. How could a student make a mistake if there was no absolute standard by which to be judged? However, at the end of that semester I had great grades in every class except English! I made a *C* in that class. How was that possible? I could not understand why my grade was a *C*. I had turned in every paper.

Several years ago I was retelling this story to Shirley and our sons. Ben said, "Dad, you don't understand this professor's philosophy very well. How could he give one student an *A*, and another a *B*. Since the professor believed that there is no standard, then everyone should be treated equally and would therefore receive the same grade! Since, according to this world view, there is no absolute standard, no reference point by which to judge, a letter grade of *C* would be the most appropriate for all students." I would like to look up the grades of all those students in his class.

The second semester, however, was quite a different story. I remember the professor, who spoke with an East European accent, telling us that we would be expected to write many essays during the semester. Then, looking us straight in the eye as she slowly pointed her long wooden pointer from student to student, she explained that there are many, many rules of punctuation and grammar and that we would be expected to know and follow each and every one! Within this English department, two views of composition were held — the new way of thinking and the old.

What about Pablo Picasso? What do we know about this man? What were his ideas and how did he express them? Picasso is considered the father of modern thinking in art. According to Dr. Schaeffer:

> Picasso then pushed [art] further. Unlike, say, Renoir, who painted his wife in such a way that she could be recognized. Picasso was seeking for a universal. As he abstracted further, one cannot tell whether his women are blondes or brunettes. This is a move towards the universal and away from the

particular. But if you go far enough, your abstracted women can become "all women" or even everything. But the difficulty is that when you get to that point the viewer has no clue what he is looking at. You have succeeded in making your own world on your canvas, and in this sense you have become god...[15]

Camus, cummings, and Picasso were all challenging the traditional view of life. They were advocating a *new way of thinking!*

What is the essence of this *new way of thinking?* It says that since there is no God, then there is no ultimate source of truth. Since there is no ultimate source of truth then there are no absolutes. Since there are no absolutes, then we live in moral relativity with no moral standards, no right from wrong. It quickly follows that there is no ultimate purpose or meaning to life. According to this view Camus was correct — life is absurd. In this *new way of thinking* anyone can make up his own world and become like God! The acceptance of this way of thinking was described in the Book of Judges as "everyone did what was right in his own eyes" (Judges 21: 25).

This *new way of thinking* is being proposed at the Presidential level by the First Lady. Historically, the next generation may look back to April, 1993, as the time when this *new way of thinking* became the official way of thinking of our country. It is a monumental move away from our Judeo-Christian heritage. It is a move toward a complete secular view of thinking. It is an all-pervasive outlook on life. It reaches out and touches every area of life. There is nothing that escapes its grasp.

This *new way of thinking* goes something like this:

> Since man evolved to his present form by the accumulation of individual, random changes preserved by natural selection, he is thought to be the highest order of animals in the evolutionary chain. From random molecules to man the progression proceeded — first from fish to amphibian, from amphibian to reptile, from reptile to mammal, and finally to the emergence of man. For this reason, man is neither separate nor unique from the animal kingdom. On the other hand, since he is now capable of

manipulating the DNA codes through conceptual understandings, man is capable of directing his own evolutionary development and destiny, and, therefore, he becomes "like God." With his new knowledge of the genetic code, all life is reduced to the complex interrelation between chemical and physical properties. Now man is reduced to nothing more than a very complex biological machine.

Since man is made of nothing but matter, it then follows that at death the highly organized biological machine simply returns to its basic elements and man disappears. There is no life after death because there is nothing more to life than matter. At death man ceases to exist. He simply enters into the cosmic darkness.

The New Age

"The new man for a new world order" is the vision of the New Age. The secular man, seen only as matter, finds a higher self in the New Age. He finds a spiritual dimension to life. However, this 'spiritual' dimension is not that of the Biblical perspective. The deception of this world view is that it draws from both the secular and the spiritual. Man becomes the center of the cosmos. Man under this new consciousness will evolve into a god himself. Unlike naturalism, the New Age perceives an invisible universe with spiritual qualities. This facet has great appeal to those disillusioned with Christianity, but are longing for a spiritual dimension to life. It is especially appealing to the secularist, because it is based upon the evolutionary premise that man has evolved. It extends the idea of evolution to include the evolution of a "new man" with a higher consciousness. The New Age man finds a spiritual dimension that removes the fear of death. Man either unifies with the "higher cosmic consciousness" or possibly returns to earth in some reincarnate form.

Though the new age may appear to be foolish and unthinkable to those working from the Biblical world view, it must not be dismissed as a contender in the cultural conflict for the minds of our children. Expressions of this view are entering our culture with great force from media, government, and educational authorities.

Is There Really a God?

The Biblical world view is based upon the existence of God while the secular view is not. The New Age is an attempt to wed the gods of Eastern mysticism and naturalism of Western thinking and thus introduces a new concept of God into our culture.

The Biblical world view understands God to be infinite and yet personal; He is beyond us and yet with us; He is all-knowing and yet knowable; He is sovereign and yet not tyrannical; God is good not evil.

By contrast, the secular world view denies the need for God. Matter takes the place of God. The universe itself becomes eternal. (In this system of thought the government usually becomes all knowing, all powerful, and all intrusive. These three characteristics — omniscient, omnipotent, and omnipresent — are attributed to God in the Biblical world view.) Since matter is all that exists and since matter is impersonal, it naturally follows that the universe too is impersonal. Because of his new ability to manipulate evolutionary direction, modern man, at the pinnacle of evolutionary development, becomes like God.

Our Responsibility

Amid the press and pressure of busy schedules, what is it that anchors us to the vision for discipling our children? When our children have reached adulthood, what is it that we want to see in them? What is it that we are praying and working to develop in their lives? What is it that we desire to impart to them?

There is no simple response to these and other similar questions. However, one thing is certain. The lives of our children must be built upon the Biblical world view. Christianity at the end of the twentieth century is losing its most fundamental struggle — the battle for the Christian mind.

As we consider equipping our children to live in a society that is becoming increasingly hostile toward Christianity, our children must be able to stand independent of the current thoughts and ideas of our culture. The apostle Paul warned us that "we are no longer to be children, tossed here and there by waves, and carried about by every wind of doctrine, by the trickery of men, by craftiness in deceitful scheming; but speaking the truth in love" (Ephesians 4: 14,15). Parents who build their families upon the Biblical world view are not easily tossed by the wind and blown in different directions. Resting our families upon the foundation of the Biblical world view allows us to see how all of life fits together.

Blaine and I were attending a convention in Minneapolis, Minnesota several years ago. During some free time we went to St. Anthony Falls, the furthermost northern point of navigation on the Mississippi River. The bedrock, the foundation of the river, was continuing to be eroded in this area by the force of the river. Many years ago the falls were further up the river. What could be done? The historic marker explained that the U.S. Corps of Engineers laid a solid foundation of cement at the base of the river and the erosion was stopped. If they had not gone into this area and laid a new foundation for the river, it would have continued to erode making it impossible for ships to navigate this portion of the river. What was the role of the Corps of Engineers? To lay a solid, strong, stable foundation.

When we consider the moral and spiritual collapse of our culture, what are we to do? David, the Psalmist, asked a similar question: *"If the foundations are destroyed, what can the righteous do"* (Psalm 11:3)? The foundation for our society for almost 1900 years has been Christianity. We are not saying that during this time all people were Christians. Neither are we saying that the world was perfect during this time in history. We must never romanticize about this. However, the Biblical world view was the base for knowing right from wrong, for knowing truth from error, and for knowing God. Purpose and meaning to life rests upon this basis.

For example, the worth and dignity of man was based upon the belief that man was created in the "image of God." This idea is unique to the Biblical world view. The Romans did not know of it. The Greeks would have never derived it. The only base that can give society a solid foundation has been eroded. Society is now in the white waters of secularism.

The true foundation has been destroyed! What are the righteous to do? Just as the U.S. Corps of Engineers went in and made a new foundation of solid concrete, God has called us as parents to lay a strong, solid Biblical base — a Biblical world view — for our children to build their lives upon. This solid base will insure that our children can navigate in and out of the culture and enable them to:

(1) stand independent of the thoughts and ideas of the culture;
(2) judge the thoughts and ideas of the culture;

(3) have a framework on which to make personal decisions: and (4) proclaim a clear, consistent presentation of the Christian world view through art, music, science and technology, government, business, philosophy, and theology to the twentieth-first century.

Unfortunately, many Christians have fragmented their lives into little compartments. Christianity is seen only as a small slice of their life. There is a separation between Christianity and the rest of life. The kind of music a person listens to, the art or movies a person watches, the political persuasion embraced, and leisure time are not seen as affected by Christianity. Christ is usually seen to affect the spiritual dimension of life, personal morality, and family life; however, the rest of life is untouched. Though this is a common view of life, it is not the Biblical world view. All aspects of life are to be under the authority of Christ. This supposed separation between the spiritual and the secular is artificial. Furthermore, it is the secular world view that propagates this wall of separation to keep its own influence over these other areas. According to the Biblical world view in addition to one's personal morality, family life and leisure time, areas like art, music, literature, science, politics, and economics — all of life— is to be under the Lordship of Jesus Christ. Absolute truth is the gauge or measure of all areas of life. Christ and the truth of Christianity provide the only absolute basis on which all of life can be evaluated and judged.

IN AS MUCH AS *there are several world views vying for the control of our culture and therefore the lives of our children; and,* FURTHERMORE, *since the Biblical world view gives the only adequate answers for a culture or a person's life,*

THEREFORE, LET US HIGHLY RESOLVE
to build our families upon the Biblical world view.

To Establish Our Children's Lives Upon Truth And Absolutes

The Road Not Taken

Two roads diverged in a yellow wood,
And sorry I could not travel both
And be one traveler, long I stood
And looked down one as far as I could
To where it bent in the undergrowth;

Then took the other, as just as fair,
And having perhaps the better claim,
Because it was grassy and wanted wear;
Though as for that the passing there
Had worn them really about the same,

And both that morning equally lay
In leaves no step had trodden black.
Oh, I kept the first for another day!
Yet knowing how way leads on to way,
I doubted if I should ever come back.

I shall be telling this with a sigh
Somewhere ages and ages hence:
Two roads diverged in a wood, and I —
I took the one less traveled by,
And that has made all the difference.[1]

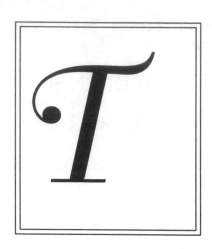wo roads diverge in a culture. At first they may appear to be the same. However, the end is quite different. Unfortunately, the most often trodden is the road to relativism; its end is destruction. The one less traveled by is based upon absolute truth and leads to fulfillment and a personal knowledge of God. The road taken by a person or people will make all the difference. Jesus explained it this way:

> Enter by the narrow gate; for the gate is wide, and the way is broad that leads to destruction, and many are those who enter by it. For the gate is small, and the way is narrow that leads to life, and few are those who find it (Matthew 7: 13-14).

The Biblical world view is based upon the existence of God while the secular view is not. The New Age is an attempt to wed the god of Eastern mysticism and naturalism of Western thinking and is therefore introducing a new concept of God into our culture.

DEUTERONOMY — *the Law*
NUMBERS — *God's Faithfulness*
LEVITICUS — *Holiness*
EXODUS — *the Law*

The Road to Relativism

"Now it came about that after the death of Joshua that the sons of Israel inquired of the Lord..." (Judges 1:1). Joshua, the great spiritual-military leader of Israel had died. Would Israel remain true to the infinite-personal God? Let us turn to the last chapter of the same book. "In those days there was no king in Israel; everyone did what was right in his own eyes" (Judges 21:25). What commentary is the author of this book giving? The book begins with the spiritual leaders inquiring of the Lord, and it ends with no spiritual leadership and the people doing what they think best. What they think best? How is this possible? God had explicitly told the people how life ought to be lived.

In the book of Exodus the Israelites were given the law of God and the institution and construction of the Tabernacle. The book of Leviticus emphasizes the theme of God's call to holiness. The principle theme of the book of Numbers is God's faithfulness and power. Then comes the book of Deuteronomy. To make it crystal clear, God goes back over the explanations to this new generation. This book includes a retelling of many of the laws given in Exodus, Leviticus, and Numbers. The way life ought to be lived is clear, detailed, and absolute. God provides a framework for living for His people. This framework is not to be thought of as just some good set of suggestions, but rather clear statements of truth, absolute truth, on which a person and people should base their life! Absolute truth is based upon the nature and character of God Himself.

In fact, the transfer of this truth was to pass from generation to generation just as it passed from Abraham, Isaac, Jacob, and Joseph — from faith to faith. Moses explains in Deuteronomy 6 that what the Israelites were to teach their children and grandchildren was what he had taught them.

Moses said in Deuteronomy 6:

> Now this is the commandment, the statues and the judgments which the Lord your God has commanded me [MOSES] to teach YOU, that you might do them in the land where you are going over to possess it, so that you and YOUR SON and YOUR GRANDSON might fear the Lord your God, to keep all His statutes and His commandments, which I command you, all the days of your life, and that your days may be prolonged. O Israel, you should listen and be careful to do it, that it may be well with you and that you may multiply greatly, just as the Lord, the God of your fathers, has promised you in a land flowing with milk and honey (1-3).

What was to be passed on? First, a personal knowledge of God, and second, a whole-hearted love of Him! This is the mark of the Christian: knowing and loving God. We can not pass on to our children and grandchildren what is not real to us.

> Hear, O Israel! The Lord is our God, the Lord is one! And *you* shall love the Lord your God with all *your* heart and with all *your* soul and with all *your* might. And these words, which I am commanding you today, shall be on *your* heart (4 - 6).

Then Moses talks about the transfer of truth from father to son.

> ... and you shall teach them diligently to your sons and shall talk of them when you sit in your house and when you walk by the way and when you lie down and when you rise up. And you shall bind them as a sign on your hand and they shall be as frontals on your forehead. And you shall write them on the doorposts of your house and on your gates (7 - 9).

Obviously, Moses was serious about this transfer of truth. Fathers were to communicate diligently and conscientiously with their children about *their* personal knowledge of the living God. Why was he being so all-inclusive in this instruction? Each generation stands at the same place of Adam and Eve — as unprogrammed man — able to choose between walking with God or walking away from Him. Fathers are to talk with the children about their walk with God. This primary responsibility was not to be delegated to others or dismissed as unimportant.

> Then it shall come about when the Lord your God brings you into the land which He swore to your fathers, Abraham, Isaac, and Jacob, to give you great and splendid cities which you did not build, and houses full of all good things which you did not fill, and hewn cisterns which you did not dig, vineyards and olive trees which you did not plant, and you shall eat and be satisfied, then watch yourself, lest you forget the Lord who brought you from the land of Egypt, out of the house of slavery (10 - 12).

Personal peace and prosperity may act like a dense fog—clouding over our minds. Moses warns them to "watch yourself, lest you forget the Lord." It seems rather impossible that they could forget the ten plagues, the parting of the Red Sea, God giving the law at Mt. Sinai, and the provision of God as they wandered in the wilderness! But God, knowing the natural tendency of the heart of man, clearly explains what to expect.

God explains that the great temptation would be to walk away from the infinite-personal God. When things return to 'normal', when the mighty time of miracles decreases and things go back to the way they were, then there will be a tendency to do what the surrounding people are doing. The natural tendency of God's people throughout history is to walk in the world view of the culture in which they are living.

> You shall fear only the Lord your God; and you shall worship Him, and swear by His name. You shall not follow other gods, any of the gods of the peoples who surround you, for the Lord your God in the midst of you is a jealous God; otherwise the anger of the Lord your God will be kindled against you, and He will wipe you off the face of the earth (13 - 15).

Before returning to the book of Judges, it is important to establish who it was that entered into God's promise and the Promised Land. The adults who had seen the ten plagues in their deliverance from Egypt and to whom the law was given had died in the wilderness. Their children had become adults and God re-explained the law to them. It was to these adults that the command to transfer truth was clearly explained in Deuteronomy 6. Moses gives the leadership to Joshua, and then he dies.

Joshua was probably in his late 20's or early 30's at the time of the exodus. He and others of his generation were certainly old enough to know personally the works of God. At the time of Moses' death Joshua was in his 70's. The next generation enters the land under Joshua's leadership and continues to see many miracles of God in its conquest. The book of Joshua catalogs this conquest. At the end of his book Joshua is 110 years old. Shortly before his death Joshua warns the elders and their children not to serve the Egyptian gods nor the gods in this new land. In his last recorded speech he says, "And if it is disagreeable in your sight to serve the Lord, choose for yourselves today whom you will serve; whether the gods which your fathers served which were beyond the River, or the gods of the Amorites in whose land you are living, but as for me and my house, we will serve the Lord... And the people answered Joshua, "...we will serve the Lord." ...And it came about after these things that Joshua the son of Nun, the servant of the Lord died, being one hundred and ten years old....And Israel served the Lord all the days of Joshua and all the days of the elders who survived Joshua, and had known all the deeds of the Lord which He had done for Israel" (Joshua 24: 15, 21, 29, 31).

Now let us return to the book of Judges. "And the people served the Lord all the days of Joshua, and all the days of the elders who survived Joshua, who had seen all the great work of the Lord which He had done for Israel. Then Joshua the son of Nun, the servant of the Lord, died at the age of one hundred and ten... And all that generation also were gathered to their fathers (Judges 2:7-8, 10a). It is reemphasized that these "had seen all the great work of the Lord which He had done for Israel."

Then we read an astonishing thing. "And there arose another generation after them who did not know the Lord, nor yet the work which He had done for Israel. Then the sons of Israel did evil in the sight of the Lord, and served the Baals (Judges 2: 10b). It is not absolutely clear as to whom this new 'generation' is, but it is most likely their own children!

THE 1ST GENERATION TO ENTER THE PROMISED LAND WAS THE CHILDREN OF THOSE DELIVERED FROM EGYPT. THEY REMEMBERED THE LORD (JUDGES 2:7). THE 2ND GENERATION (THE CHILDREN OF THE 1ST GENERATION) DID NOT KNOW THE LORD, NOR DID THEY KNOW OF HIS WORKS (JUDGES 2:10). THE 3RD GENERATION DID WHATEVER WAS RIGHT IN IT'S OWN EYES (JUDGES 17:6 AND 21:25).

God's plan was for the parents to transfer to their children and grandchildren the truth that they had learned from Moses about who God is. However, we read that although the first generation remembered the Lord, the second did not know Him or His works. Their basis for life was gone. Although they may have followed some of the moral guidelines, they were an empty shell. Next, a new generation would be raised with their lives setting upon this empty shell. The rug of an absolute moral standard to give guidance and direction to ethical choices was pulled out from under them. They must decide for themselves what is right or wrong. They became a ship without a rudder in a sea of moral relativism.

This never should have happened! The adults of Moses' generation were delivered from Egypt, but because of unbelief they did not enter the Promised Land. Joshua's generation, the children of Moses' generation, were the youth who were delivered from Egypt and the same generation to enter into the promised land. That generation knew the Lord. Their children, the grandchildren of Moses' generation, however, did not know the Lord, nor did they know of His works. The next generation, the great-grandchildren of Moses' generation, did whatever was right in its own eyes (Judges 17:6 and 21:25).

God had told them what to do. They had seen His mighty acts. He had warned them of what could happen as they began to settle in the land, and it did. Though it seems impossible, this same parallel is seen over and over again in history. It stands as a warning to our generation.

Moral and ethical decisions made apart from the personal knowledge of the personal-infinite God are relative. Without God there exists no absolute reference point. God has given us a gauge with which we are to measure thoughts and ideas. Man has a standard by which to judge the thoughts and intents of his own life as well as society. They are not simply a set of rules to be memorized and followed. They are so much more. Because they are His Word, they are a reflection of His character.

Naturalism leads to the Road to Relativism Today

The road to relativism starts when a person or people suppress the truth by not honoring God as being God (Romans 1). When He is no longer acknowledged as the Creator, then the supernatural dimension of life is lost. This vacuum is replaced by humanism. Man, reasoning from himself apart from divine revelation, devises all sorts of speculations about life. *Who Am I? Where am I from?* and *Where am I going?* The answers to these questions are now up for grabs. While working from the absolutes of the Judeo-Christian world view, we can find good and sufficient answers to these and other questions. However, working from the humanistic base, man's nature is clouded within the mystery of his psyche. Man's origin is now hidden behind billions of years of speculation. Man's destiny is questioned, and his dignity is lost. As the secular world view began to encroach upon Western culture it said that there was no need for a *personal* God. Then it pushed further. Instead of man being created in God's image, the secular world view explained that the notion of God was simply an imagination created within the mind of man. At the end of the 20th century according to the naturalistic world view, the Judeo-Christian belief in God is thought to be just as irrational as the Greek myths. With God now removed from our society, all frameworks are removed. All boundaries are gone, and man is free to do whatever seems right in his own eyes. Unfortunately, relativism will not lead to further freedom, but to hopelessness, and hopelessness to despair.

Moral and Ethical Implications

What is it that guides and directs man in making moral and ethical decisions? "How do we know what is right and wrong for ourselves as individuals and for our society?" asks Jerram Barrs. "The Christian answer," he explains, "is simply that God's existence and character provide a final and absolute difference between good and evil, that we are at home ultimately in a moral universe, so we have an absolute basis for morality against which we may judge society."[2] The Biblical world view offers a drastically different set of ideas regarding morality and ethics when compared to the secular or New Age views. Man working out of the Biblical view understands that values come from God. They are a reflection of His Divine nature and character. Because God is eternal and unchanging, the values derived from Him are also eternal and unchanging. The person whose life is based upon the Biblical world view is established upon truth. Truth provides an absolute moral standard for measuring personal decisions and for judging cultural decisions. We can, therefore, check not only our personal decisions, but also the cultural ideas against the character of God and His truth.

Individual decisions are not simply personal preferences. Neither are they an adherence to a certain political perspective. Christians can speak with authority knowing that the standard is not man-made, and therefore finite, but rather based upon the infinite God, and therefore absolute.

Properly interpreted and applied Christianity is not reduced to a moral code, but rather the moral code points us to the infinite-personal God. This idea can not be overemphasized. The road map of the Biblical world view leads both to moral behavior and to the infinite-personal God.

T h e   B i b l i c a l   W o r l d   V i e w

INFINITE-PERSONAL GOD → ULTIMATE TRUTH → ABSOLUTES → MORAL UNIVERSE

THE BIBLICAL WORLD VIEW STARTS WITH THE INFINITE-PERSONAL GOD. ULTIMATE TRUTH NATURALLY FOLLOWS FROM THIS START. ULTIMATE TRUTH PROVIDES A BASIS FOR ABSOLUTES. ABSOLUTES FORM A FRAMEWORK OF RIGHT AND WRONG.

The secular man, by contrast, reasons that values are man-made. Since all life has evolved, it naturally follows that values themselves can evolve, and are therefore relative. Since values are relative, they must change with the circumstances or as culture changes. In fact, changes in values become necessary. Any fixed set of values, according to this view, impede progress. Anyone holding to a fixed set of moral beliefs is seen as intolerant.

If man is a machine or animal, as the secular world view claims, then it is meaningless even to speak of there being a right or wrong, or good or evil for that matter. Why should man, now scientifically known to be an animal, be held responsible for moral behavior? A dog is not held responsible for killing a cat or a cat for killing a bird.

T h e   S e c u l a r   W o r l d   V i e w

NO GOD → NO ULTIMATE TRUTH → RELATIVISM → ARBITRARY RIGHT/WRONG

THE SECULAR WORLD VIEW MUST BEGIN WITH MAN. ULTIMATE TRUTH AND AN ABSOLUTE MORAL STANDARD DO NOT EXIST. MORALITY AND ETHICS ARE BASED UPON RELATIVISM, AND THEREFORE THEY ARE ARBITRARY AND EVOLVING.

Though the secular view may say that man is just an animal, that does not make it true. This map does not fit true human nature. Man is a moral creature, and to say otherwise does not change who man is!

With the New Age man comes a slight variation from the secular view. Those who have evolved into the 'highest consciousness' should be given the right to choose which values the culture accepts. This new cultural elite has a duty to transform morality and ethics to prepare the global family for the "new world utopian order." For example, the notion of *traditional family values* to the New Age and secular man stands in sharp contrast to that of the person working out of the Biblical base. Both define the attributes of "a family" from their world view, their perspective. The recent ongoing debate regarding *what is a family* clearly shows that ideas have consequences. Ethical and moral decisions are derived from world views!

Culture is in conflict today because the basic ideas, the world views, are in a great struggle for dominance. The resolve to help our children carefully choose the correct world view is not an option. Ethics and morality not based upon a complete world view picture will not withstand the cultural pressures. During the 1950's adults tried to hang on to Christian morality without accepting the totality of the Biblical world view. People wanted the morality without submitting to the infinite-personal God. The consequence was that with the pressures of the 1960's cultural morality crumbled. There was no base, no foundation, on which to build morality.

When God was banned from our public life during the 1960's and 1970's, virtue, truth, and moral absolutes vanished. Edith Schaeffer writes:

> People today are all mixed up in twisted ideas. They live in a welter of garbled voices, looking for directions from papers that come floating down like Alice in Wonderland's cards, scattered like blown leaves all about her. Although these papers are in different languages, from different thought-forms, different philosophies all say that there is no truth and no absolute upon which to live, no base or any choice of a moral standard. So whether one reads the papers upside down, left to right, knows one word in three, it doesn't matter. There'll be a new wind in a few days to blow more into one's head. Perhaps you can even stop looking for papers among the falling leaves. Just turn to the last piece of television advice, given in the most colorful or unforgettable way — whatever has stuck in the memory. One way is as good as any other! All law is obsolete. There are no more standards.[3]

IN AS MUCH AS *the school, the church, the neighborhood, and even some of our own relatives no longer embrace the common set of ideas based upon the Bible; and,*
FURTHERMORE, *hoping that our children pick up bits and pieces of the Biblical world view from here and there by chance may have worked a century ago, but certainly not in this culture;*

THEREFORE, LET US HIGHLY RESOLVE to establish our children's lives upon the road of truth and absolutes which lead in one direction to a proper base for making moral and ethical decisions in their personal lives and in the other direction leading to a proper relationship with the infinite-personal God.

To Equip Our Children To Reason

When I was a child, I used to speak as a child, think as a child, reason as a child; when I became a man, I did away with childish things.
— I Corinthians. 13: 11

"Come now, and let us reason together," says the Lord.
— Isaiah 1:18

Most behaviorists are committed to [the ideas of B.F. Skinner]. Man is accepted as a machine and he is treated as a machine…[Man] has no soul, he has no mind; he neither initiates, originates nor creates.[1]
— Francis Schaeffer

"Luke, trust your feelings … Use the Force, Luke … Let go … Trust me…" implores Obi-Wan ….[2]

"Tell me why!" demands Luke.
"Why? Never ask why?" chides Yoda.[3]
— George Lucas

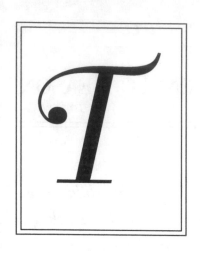

o properly understand the resolve to teach our children to reason, it is necessary to place it into the flow of history. During the 1600's *revelation* was considered the ultimate source of truth and knowledge. God through the Scripture has revealed Himself to man. It was not that people during this time did not use reason or express emotion. Rather, these two human functions were under the umbrella of *Divine revelation.* The Biblical world view was understood to give man both adequate and sufficient answers to the basic questions of life. Revelation was the gauge by which reason and feelings were measured. The ability to reason is God-given. When it stands in its proper place under the umbrella of revelation, this ability is of great value to man. During this time in history the Bible gave an absolute reference point on which to base reason and emotion.

T H E F L O W O F T H O U G H T			
REVELATION ➤ REASON ➤ ROMANTICISM ➤ NON REASON			
1600's	1700's	1800's	1900's

The 1700's left revelation and enthroned *reason* as the goddess of worship. When man reasons apart from God and His Word, it leads to confusion and empty speculations. Adam and Eve, reasoning apart from God's Word, ushered humanity into this state of confusion. During the

1700's, man was left alone to find for himself all that he needed to know. However, because man is not all-knowing, he is unable to draw an adequate map of life.

Reason was toppled during the 1800's. *Romanticism* rose to the top. Man would escape from reason and turn to feelings and experience. However, since feelings and experiences are as changing as the tide, these too would fail!

By the 1900's, both *reason* and *romanticism* had failed to find the proper place for man in the universe. When man threw off *revelation*, *reason* and *romanticism* had no reference point to guide the culture. What was left? Now humanism had almost run its course. Having left *revelation* modern man was left to himself to draw his own map in an attempt to find the basic answers to the essential questions of life: *Who am I? Where am I from?* and *Where am I going?*

Where has this departure from his Creator left man? *Modernism* is the belief that there is no God. With no God, man is only left with naturalism. *Naturalism* is, of course, the belief that matter and energy are all there really is. There is nothing more fundamental or basic. Man, thinking that he could reason apart from divine revelation, sought to find his place in the universe. In his attempt, he found the map had brought him to his final destination. Man is just a collection of molecules, and life becomes meaningless and absurd. This hopelessness can be seen and heard quite easily in modern popular art or music.

Man now has his back against the wall. During the 20th century we find humanism between a rock and a hard place. What is man to do? Is he to return to a proper balance between reason and feelings under the authority of revelation? Or will he push further in the secular direction?

The secular choices are somewhat limited. First, he can put a good face on it and simply say that even though life has no meaning, "I will act as though it does!" Second, he can try to fill up his life with things to deaden the pain of a meaningless existence. Third, he can end his life in suicide. In all these choices reasoning is discarded altogether. Two paths are now set before man.

Chicken Plays the Star-Spangled Banner

First, man becomes merely an animal to be conditioned or a machine to be programmed; man becomes a robot. Man moves beyond true freedom and personal dignity. His behavior becomes determined either chemically, psychologically or educationally.

These ideas have been forced on our culture during this century. A leading proponent of this view was the late behavioral psychologist and author B. F. Skinner. He studied the learning of animals and applied these principles to people. Just how effective are these techniques?

Going to the state fair was a yearly tradition of my family. I remember the livestock buildings as my favorite. I loved seeing the great variety of animals groomed to perfection. Outside the poultry building were several cages containing chickens. These were not just ordinary chickens; they were very special. The sign above the cages read "CHICKEN PLAYS STAR-SPANGLED BANNER." For 5¢ a xylophone would drop from the side, and the chicken would play our national anthem.

I remember reaching into my pocket and feeling the nickel. I hesitated. My palms began to be moist. Could it be true? Was it possible that a chicken could play this song I had been taught to love? Should I place my money into the slot to find out? I looked up at my parents for their approval.

However, before I had a chance to pull out my coin to find out, another person pushed ahead of me. To my amazement this chicken was able to peck out on the xylophone the melody to this dearly beloved song. Was this chicken a musician? To a five-year-old it surely was.

It was not until many years later, however, that I learned just how it was possible. The whole musical piece was broken into bits and pieces, that is, into small increments. The chicken was then conditioned one note one at a time to "play" the tune. For example, if the chicken pecked a "C", then it was given a reward (a kernel of corn). If it pecked any other note, then it was not given a reward. After the chicken "learned" or was conditioned to peck the "C", the reward was gradually removed. To receive the corn now it was necessary for the chicken to peck a "C" followed by an "A". This process was continued until the chicken was conditioned to play the entire melody. All the while, the bits and pieces of the whole, the so-called increments, were continually reviewed.

There are several questions I would now like to ask that chicken about his ability to play THE STAR-SPANGLED BANNER. Could he peck out any other song? Does he think that he is any closer to becoming a musician than before he was conditioned to "play" this piece? Has he developed perfect pitch or for that matter relative pitch? Does he believe that being programmed to play a piece is the same thing as becoming a concert pianist?

The teaching-training model applied to the chicken is called BEHAVIORISM. It has been used to train animals to perform quite a number of tricks. It is frightening to realize that the use of this method has not been limited to animals.

This educational model, based upon the thoughts and ideas of B.F. Skinner, is being used by the "New Elite" to manipulate and control the people of our culture. The behaviorist reduces man to nothing more than molecules or a machine. Dr. Schaeffer explains that according to the behaviorist view, "Not only does man have no soul, he has no mind; he neither initiates, originates nor creates."[4]

Could what Skinner suggest ever be implemented into our culture? Are these behavioral ideas just in some abstract form? Schaeffer goes on to say, "Most behaviorists are committed to [the ideas of B. F. Skinner]. Man is accepted as a machine and he is treated as a machine. Such professionals are there by the hundreds, some of them with understanding, some of them with power... In some places they control the educational processes down into the earliest days of school. A brilliant girl teaching psychology in a social science department in a British university was forced to choose whether to teach in a behavioristic structure or to leave the university. The girl walked out. She had to. Behaviorism is not something that we can simply dismiss. Its power is too great."[5]

We are not questioning the power of behaviorism. Obviously, it is a very powerful technique to train an animal. However, we are questioning its underlying assumptions. To answer this question we must return to our understanding of world views. Is man an animal or a machine, or is man unique from both? If the secular position of man is correct, then it would be appropriate to program or condition him. If the Biblical view is correct, the use of behavior modification techniques on people eradicates everything that makes human life valuable from the standpoint of what God meant us to be as men in His image.

The Biblical view of man is that he was created in the image of God. This view of man has resulted in the overwhelming worth and dignity of the individual that has been unique to Western civilization. The humanistic conclusion is the complete opposite! Man, according to this view, has no dignity. Twentieth century man is in a dilemma. He wants and needs to believe he has dignity and worth, and yet his world view denounces such a possibility.

It is sometimes tempting as a parent to wish that we could raise or teach our children by simply giving them a "right choice" pill. If this pill would enable them always to make the right choice throughout life, wouldn't it be a lot easier? Yes, but would it be right? While this kind of possibility might simplify life for parents, it would certainly not be consistent with the Biblical world view.

Before the creation of man, God could have placed an electric force field around the Tree of the Knowledge of Good and Evil. If Adam or Eve had tried to approach the Tree, they would have received an electric shock. They would probably have tried to approach the Tree from a variety of directions. Each time, however, they would have been shocked. Eventually they would have been trained not to come near the tree. Why did God not do this? Because Adam and Eve were people — not animals. According to the Biblical world view we live in a cause-and-effect world. This is true in the physical, the moral and spiritual realms. There are consequences to ideas and behaviors. God said to Adam and Eve "From any tree of the garden you may eat freely, but from the tree of the knowledge of good and evil you shall not eat, FOR IN THE DAY THAT YOU EAT FROM IT YOU SHALL SURELY DIE (Genesis 2:16,17, emphasis added). He explicitly gave both the command and its consequence. With most commands given by God in Scripture He tells us *why*. Behaviorism is rarely concerned with the *why*; rather, the focus is only on the external behavior. Man is reduced to biology and nothing more.

The Bible makes it clear that man was not created as animals to be conditioned or as robots to be programmed. In *Genesis in Space and Time* Dr. Schaeffer writes, "The machine (for example, the solar system) can obey God mechanically; when it does, it is doing all that God meant it to do. The far-flung system of the universe operates, much of it, as a great machine; and as such it fulfills its purpose. That is all it was meant to do. But man is a different being, made in a different circle of creation. He is to love God, not mechanically, but by the wonder of choice. Here stands an unprogrammed part of creation — unprogrammed chemically or psychologically — real man in a real history, a wonder in the midst of a world of uniformity of cause and effect. In the flow of history, man is brought face to face with that for which he has been made — face to face in a loving relationship to the God who is there."[6]

The Force Be With You

A second choice lies before man at the end of this century. Man could deny reason and revelation and return to experience and feelings with a New Age twist. Man, however, becomes irrational in this system as he entrusts himself to the impersonal Force of the Eastern religions.

The most dramatic and persuasive introduction of the Eastern pantheistic world view came from the multimillion dollar movie series "Star Wars" by George Lucas. "Luke, trust your feelings,"[7] exhorts Obi-Wan. The old Jedi Master instructs his student Luke Skywalker not to rely upon his reason or his sense, but rather his inner touch with a higher reality — the Force. The scene is the one in which the young Western-looking boy is learning to fight, using a light sabre. To test Luke's inner connection with the Force, Obi-Wan gives him a helmet that covers his eyes as he practices. To Luke's surprise he actually hits his mark. In this movie Luke is being taught that rationality and senses are actually obstructing the Force. Later in the story the rebellion is about to be crushed by the Death Star. However, in a dramatic segment the same young fighter pilot engages the two meter target to destroy the Death Star at an incredible speed with the use of the most advanced computer tracking technology. Within just seconds of releasing the missiles, a spirit voice guiding him says, "Use the Force, Luke ... Let go ... trust me."[8] Will the young pilot trust his fighter training and sophisticated technology or will he trust the Force? He shuts down his on-board computer tracking system and he relies upon the Force to direct his behavior. He releases the missiles. Within seconds the Death Star dramatically explodes by a direct hit guided not be reason, not by the senses, not by technology, but by the Force.

In the sequel the young boy is ready for his advanced training in Zen Buddhism. He searches and finds the Jedi Master Yoda, a strange looking creature with great ability to use the Force. At one point Luke in frustration demands of the Master:

"Tell me why!"

"Why? Never ask why!" chides Yoda.

"You must unlearn what you have learned."[9]

Many millions of people coming with a heritage of the Western Judeo-Christian or secular world view were powerfully introduced to the Eastern pantheistic world view in this most dramatic way — a powerful presentation of the false god of Eastern thought and a false view of man. There is an interesting observation about this whole episode: *those displaying the greatest rationality and thought were actually robots!*

Be ready! Three more episodes from the GOSPEL ACCORDING TO LUCAS on the Force philosophy of life are soon to be released. EPISODE I: THE PHANTOM MENACE takes us deep into the inner sanctum of the Jedi Temple to instruct us in the religious nature of the Force. These movies have and will continue to dramatically shape the thinking of the Western culture. Hollywood is such a powerful force. Producers and directors are attempting to usher in their theology through dazzling cinematography.

Treating People As People

Where does this *new way of thinking* leave man? Modern man loses his dignity either way he goes. Down the secular path he becomes no more than a robot. Down the Eastern path man is reduced to electrochemical elements in search of the Force. The end is actually the same. Man is not man. According to Skinner "to man *qua* man we readily say good riddance."[10]

The resolve to build our families upon the Biblical world view certainly means that our children are reasoning from that view — not simply as programmed robots. It means that we teach our children not only to understand that the whole of life is based upon the Biblical base, but also to equip them to be able to reason from that base. In contrast to the behavioral view, the Biblical world view declares that man has a soul, he has a mind; he initiates, originates, and creates. It will do our children little good to know about the Biblical world view if they cannot reason consistently for themselves based upon that view. On the other hand, if a person is able to reason, but does so on a base different than the Biblical one, he will not find adequate answers to life's basic questions. Our children must be able to reason, and this reasoning must be based upon the Biblical world view.

Research suggests that reasoning strategies progress through several stages. Each stage has its own unique characteristics of reasoning. Michael Bond's beloved character Paddington Bear wins the hearts of young and old alike because of Bond's understanding of children. Paddington's comical adventures erupt because of his childlike reasonings. The following episode is taken from *Paddington Goes to School*:

> "Good-morning," he said. "I take it you're one Brown, P?"
>
> "One *brown Pea?*" repeated Paddington in surprise. He gave the man a hard stare. "No, I'm not. I'm Paddington Brown."
>
> "Er ... that's really what I was asking," he said nervously. "If you hurry you'll just be in time for the roll."
>
> Paddington licked his lips. A roll sounded a very good way in which to start the day. "I think I shall enjoy that."
>
> "Now," Mr. Eustace called ... "I assume I have your permission to take the roll?"
>
> Anxious to make a good impression on his first day, Paddington busied himself behind his desk lid. "I shan't be a moment, Mr. Eustace," he called. "I've nearly finished. I've got over thirty-three already!"
>
> "Over thirty-three?" repeated the form-mast In surprise.
>
> "That's right," said Paddington ... "Marmalade sandwiches ... I'm afraid I didn't bring any rolls ..."
>
> Marmalade sandwiches!" sputtered Mr. Eustace. He bounded from the platform all thought of checking the list of those present driven from his mind as he peered inside Paddington's desk.[11]

Every parent of young children can document many such similar circumstances. It was an early morning in late November in Dallas. Blaine was a young child at the time. He came running into our bedroom saying "It's Christmas! It's Christmas! Come look out the window. It's Christmas!" Well, we did and guess what we saw? It was not Santa Claus. Rather it was snowing! Blaine, who was about four at the time, had associated Christmas with snowing and wrongly concluded that since it was snowing it must be Christmas. Was he reasoning correctly? Of course not. However, was he reasoning as most four year old children? Yes!

The apostle Paul makes an interesting statement regarding speaking, thinking, and reasoning. He says that, "When I was a child, I used to *speak* as a child, *think* as a child, *reason* as a child; when I became a man, I did away with childish things" (I Corinthians 13: 11, emphasis added). Children do reason differently than adults. It seems to be part of growing up. However, studies indicate that children are taking longer and longer to move from childish reasoning to adult thought. While the ages of transition from stage to stage may vary, it appears that children do not jump or reverse stages. Although childish reasoning brings laughs as in Paddington Bear, it reaps havoc in a real culture. People reasoning at the childish level will not understand double meanings but will take words at their simplest, face value meaning. The movement out of childish reasoning is necessary in order to understand the meaning behind the many messages being rained down onto our culture from a variety of viewpoints. In order to understand the implications, the thoughts and ideas, behind what a person is saying, the hearer must be using abstract reasoning.

Research studies show various trends of movement from childish to adult levels of reasoning. The youngest ages reported [12] indicate that children being taught at home begin to reason abstractly between nine and ten. Children being taught in tradition institutional [13] settings, whether private or public, seem to make this transition between 15 -20 years of age. Several studies show quite disturbing results. For example, one study [14] found that *only 30% of high school seniors were reasoning at the abstract level! Reasoning from assumptions requires abstract reasoning. Therefore, seventy percent of the students in this study would not be capable of reasoning from assumptions!*

The Development of Reasoning

What is necessary to encourage children to move from childish reasoning? The answer to this question, though not simple, is understandable. There are four factors [15] affecting this change. Those factors are maturation, first hand experiences, verbal interaction, and unexpected events.[16]

Maturation

Maturation refers to the process of maturing. According to Dr. John Renner and Dr. Edmund Marek, researchers at the University of Oklahoma in their book *The Learning Cycle* explain "physiological maturation of the nervous system ... plays an indispensable role in promoting intellectual development."[17] Though the ages of maturation vary from child to child, the passing from stage to stage appears to be constant. Jumping or reversing stages does not seem to occur. Proper diet, rest, and exercise certainly play a role in this development as well.

First Hand Experiences

Touching, smelling, seeing, hearing, and tasting are all part of *physical experiences* that greatly profit a child who is reasoning at the childish level. Young children need to interact with objects. Describing, comparing, and contrasting the properties of objects will help facilitate reasoning. For example, allowing your child the opportunity to change the shape of an object in order to see if there is a corresponding change in its amount teaches cause and effect relationships crucial for children learning to reason. One study [18] even indicates that learners using adult reasoning patterns have fewer misconceptions of a concept if the learning experience is first initiated at the concrete level rather than at the abstract level.

Verbal Interaction

Normal conversations between parents and children promote intellectual development. Isolating children or having them work independently from adult conversations for long periods of time does not. What is meant by "normal conversation"? Topics range freely from work, the family, birth, growing up, to death. Such conversations include plans for the future and puzzling over such diverse topics as the shapes of roofs or chairs to the nature of God. Children are probably asking more questions than they are answering. In many conversations the children are actively struggling to understand a new idea or the meaning of an unfamiliar word. Going to museums, libraries, fire stations, concert halls, and historic sights all contribute to fostering opportunities for verbal interaction. Reading the Bible and excellent literature also provide openings for natural conversations and questions.

The Unexpected

"I didn't expect that to happen" is the comment by a person ready to make a change in his thinking. When there is a mismatch between what was expected and what actually happens, learning and reasoning are greatly enhanced. Though unexpected events are usually dependent upon some experience and/or verbal interaction, this mismatch is what causes movement from one stage of intellectual development to another.

Because school classrooms tend to limit these last three factors, it will be necessary for parents with children in school to provide these kinds of experiences at home. Those families teaching their children at home must not through intimidation or modeling try to import the classroom into their home. Firsthand experiences coupled with verbal interaction which produce an unexpected event, promote intellectual growth and reasoning. When your child exclaims, "I didn't expect that!" you can know learning and intellectual growth are taking place.

The Master Teacher

The world knows that in all recorded history there has never been anyone like Jesus of Nazareth. Visit any part of the world today and talk to people of all cultures. If they know anything of the facts, they acknowledge that there has never been a teacher like Jesus.

Since Jesus is the greatest teacher in history, it is important for us to examine the way He taught His disciples and incorporate His principles into our teaching as best we can. How did Jesus teach His disciples? How did He introduce abstract ideas to them? What impact did His way of teaching have upon them? What wisdom can we gain for teaching our children as a result of observing Him teach His disciples?

Francis and Edith Schaeffer, in their book *Everybody Can Know*, place us in the appropriate setting to observe Jesus teaching His disciples:

> Imagine an extremely large crowd following Jesus and the apostles out on the grassy hills about the lake, you must not imagine just fifty or a hundred people. This time we know how many there were in the "multitude", because we are told that there were at least five thousand. What a crowd! Instead of chasing them away, Jesus welcomed them, and spoke to

them about the things of God, and healed those who were ill. When the sun began to cast long shadows, as it does in the late afternoon, the twelve apostles came a little anxiously to Jesus and said something like this: 'You better send these crowds away now to the towns and villages around here, because we're in a desert place and there is nowhere to get food.' Can you imagine what Jesus answered? He said, 'You give them something to eat.' [19]

What do we learn from observing the teaching of Jesus as recorded by John in the sixth chapter of his gospel? Take a few minutes to read it. As you read, mark the major sections of this chapter, make a list of the main ideas of each. What do you think are the key verses? As you begin reading, ask God to give you understanding of this most important chapter.

We hope that your study was beneficial. This passage is composed of three major sections. In the first section, verses 1-21, Jesus performs two of His many miracles: the feeding of the five thousand and the calming of the great storm. In the second section, verses 22-59, Jesus gives a most important teaching. The third section, verses 60-71, tells of the responses of the followers of Jesus.

What is the major teaching of this chapter? What is Jesus communicating? Jesus gives us the key to understanding this chapter in verse 35:

> Jesus said to them, "I am the bread of life; he who comes to Me shall not hunger, and he who believes in Me shall never thirst."

Go back and reread the chapter. Look for the teaching strategy Jesus used to bring the disciples to the understanding that He is the "Bread of Life." What was the purpose of feeding the 5000? Was it to meet the physical needs of the people? Yes! But there is more. How did Jesus use this circumstance to teach something of who He is?

Imagine the excitement and enthusiasm of the apostles and disciples as Jesus multiplied the few loaves and fish. In addition, there is evidence (see Matthew 14:19) that Jesus actually used the apostles to carry out this magnificent miracle. This is one event that will never be forgotten.

Was this what the disciples had expected Jesus to do? What affect would this experience have had on the disciples? How were they prepared for the teaching Jesus was about to give?

Now the disciples were ready for the formal teaching — the great discourse on the Bread of Life. This is one of the great "I AM" statements recorded in the book of John. The teaching sequence was carefully chosen by Jesus. The formal teaching is proceeded by a firsthand experience by both the twelve and the many followers of Jesus. However, Jesus does not leave this experience just as some academic theological exercise. He asks for a response; that is, He seeks the hearers to apply His teaching.

Jesus uses a strategy for teaching that first draws His students into a direct, first-hand experience of the principle (verses 1-21). This is followed by the formal teaching of the principle (verse 22-59). It is here that He filled in what was vital for them to know. This information was based upon their previous experience. Finally, He leads them to apply the principle to their own lives (verses 60-67).

What does this mean as we teach our children? Using materials and basic directions provided by us, children should first experience the concept to be learned through hands-on activities. Next, we should formally teach our children the concept inherent in the initial experience. It is during this phase that we introduce the language or terminology of the concept. To complete the teaching, our children should then be led to apply the newly explained concept in several different ways. They might engage in additional hands-on activities, work problems, answer questions, pursue individual investigations, and/or read about the uses and further descriptions of the concept. This phase leads children to use the principle or idea they have just learned.

These three phases — *experiencing, teaching,* and *applying* the principle — used by Jesus to teach the twelve will provide structure to our teaching and at the same time provide a greater degree of understanding for our children. It is not coincidental that research studies during this century have shown this type of instruction to be the very best for truly understanding what is being taught. Real learning is then taking place!

Consequences of a Non-reasoning Culture

What are the consequences of a society that continues to reason like

Paddington Bear? A person reasoning at the childish level is not able to understand the philosophical presuppositions behind competing systems of thought. If a nation were made up predominately of adults reasoning at this level, it would be vulnerable to great deception and control by those dispensing the information to the people of that society. Symbolisms would be misunderstood and philosophies seen as irrelevant. The adult population would not be able to "read between the lines" to understand the subtle implications. Lies could then be substituted for Truth.

C.S. Lewis, in his book *The Silver Chair*, describes a people under such an enchantment:

> "Who's there?" shouted the three travellers. "I am the Warden of the Marches of Underland, and with me stand a hundred Earthmen in arms," came the reply. "Tell me quickly who you are and what is your errand in the Deep Realm?"
>
> "We fell down by accident," said Puddleglum, truthfully enough.
>
> "Many fall down, and few return to the sunlit lands," said the voice...While he said these words there was a noise like a soft explosion and immediately a cold light, grey with a little blue in it, flooded the cavern....
>
> "March," said the Warden...
>
> The cold light came from a large ball on the top of a long pole, ... By its cheerless rays they could see that they were in a natural cavern...
>
> It was full of a dim, drowsy radiance...[20]

Later in the story the two children and the Marshwiggle reach the Prince and release him. But before they can escape, they are confronted with the evil witch:

> "How now, my lord Prince," she [the witch] said. "Has your nightly fit not yet come upon you, or is it over so soon? Why stand you here unbound? Who are these aliens? And is it they who have destroyed the chair which was your only safety!"

Prince Rilian shivered as she spoke to him. And no wonder: it is not easy to throw off in half an hour an enchantment which has made one a slave for ten years. Then, speaking with a great effort, he said:

"Madam, there will be no more need of that chair. And you, who have told me a hundred times how deeply you pitied me for the sorceries by which I was bound, will doubtless hear with joy that they are now ended for ever...."

Now the Witch said nothing at all, but moved gently across the room, always keeping her face and eyes very steadily towards the Prince. When she had come to a little ark set in the wall not far from the fireplace, she opened it, and took out first a handful of a green powder. This she threw on the fire. It did not blaze much, but a very sweet and drowsy smell came from it. And all through the conversation which followed, that smell grew stronger, and filled the room, and made it harder to think. Secondly, she took out a musical instrument rather like a mandolin. She began to play it with her fingers — a steady, monotonous thrumming that you didn't notice after a few minutes. But the less you noticed it, the more it got into your brain and your blood. This also made it hard to think. After she had thrummed for a time (and the sweet smell was now strong) she began speaking in a sweet, quiet voice.

"Narnia?" she said. "Narnia? I have often heard your Lordship utter that name in your ravings. Dear Prince, you are very sick. There is no land called Narnia."

"Yes there is though, Ma'am," said Puddleglum. "You see, I happened to have lived there all my life."

"Indeed," said the Witch. "Tell me where that country is?"

"Up there," said Puddleglum, stoutly, pointing overhead. "I —I don't know exactly where."

"How?" said the Queen, with a kind, soft, musical laugh, "Is there a country up among the stones and mortar of the roof?"

"No," said Puddleglum, struggling a little to get his breath. "It's in Overworld."

"And what, or where, pray is the -how do you call it *Overworld*?"

"Oh don't be so silly," said Scrubb, who was fighting hard against the enchantment of the sweet smell and the thrumming....

Puddleglum was still fighting hard. "I don't know rightly what you all mean by a world," he said, talking like a man who hasn't enough air. "But you can play that fiddle till your fingers drop off, and still you won't make me forget Narnia; and the whole Overworld too. ...But I know I was there once. I've seen the sky full of stars. I've seen the sun coming up out of the sea of a morning and sinking behind the mountains at night. And I've seem him up in the midday sky when I couldn't look at him for brightness."...

Then came the Witch's voice, cooing softly like the voice of a wood-pigeon from the high elms in an old garden at three o'clock in the middle of a sleepy, summer afternoon; and said:

"What is this sun that you all speak of? Do you mean anything by the word?"

"Yes, we jolly well do," said Scrubb.

"Can you tell me what it's like?" asked the Witch (thrum, thrum, thrum, went the strings).

"Please it your Grace," said the Prince, very coldly and politely. "You see that lamp. It is round and yellow and gives light to the whole room; and hangeth moreover from the roof. Now that thing which we call the sun is like the lamp, only far greater and brighter. It giveth light to the whole Overworld and hangeth in the sky."

"Hangeth from what, my lord?" asked the Witch; and then, while they were all still thinking how to answer her, she added, with another of her soft, silver laughs. "You see? When you try to think out clearly what this sun must be, you cannot tell me. You can only tell me it is like the lamp. Your sun is a dream; and there is nothing in that dream that was not copied from the lamp. The lamp is the real thing; the sun is but a tale, a children's story."

"Yes, I see now," said Jill in a heavy, hopeless tone. "It must be so." While she said this, it seemed to her to be very good sense.

Slowly and gravely the Witch repeated, "There is no sun." And they all said nothing. She repeated, in a softer and deeper voice. "There is no sun." After a pause, and after a struggle in their minds, all four of them said together. "You are right. There is no sun." It was such a relief to give in and say it.

"There never was a sun," said the Witch.

"No. There never was a sun," said the Prince, and the Marsh-wiggle, and the children.

For the last few minutes Jill had been feeling that there was something she must remember at all costs. And now she did. But it was dreadfully hard to say it. She felt as if huge weights were laid on her lips. At last, with an effort that seemed to take all the good out of her, she said:

"There's Aslan."

"Aslan?" said the Witch, quickening ever so slightly the pace of her thrumming. "What a pretty name! What does it mean?"

He is the great Lion who called us out of our own world," said Scrubb, "and sent us into this place to find Prince Rilian."

What is a lion?" asked the Witch.

"Oh hang it all!" said Scrubb. "Don't you know? How can we describe it to her? Have you ever seen a cat?"

"Surely," said the Queen. "I love cats."

"Well a lion is a little bit — only a little bit, mind you — like a huge cat — with a mane. At least, it's not like a horse's mane, you know, it's more like a judge's wig. And it's yellow. And terrifically strong."

The Witch shook her head. "I see," she said, "that we should do no better with your lion, as you call it, than we did with your sun. You have seen lamps, and so you imagined a bigger and better lamp and called it the sun. You've seen cats, and it's to so called a *lion*. Well, 'tis a pretty make-believe, though to say truth, it would suit you all better if you were younger. And look how you can put nothing into your make-believe without copying it from the real world, this world of mine, which is the only world.... There is no Narnia, no Overworld, no sky, no sun, no Aslan. And now, to bed all. And let us begin a wiser life tomorrow. But first, to bed; to sleep; deep sleep, soft pillows, sleep without foolish dreams."[21]

If several generations of people are treated as machines and are programmed as such or viewed as animals and conditioned as such, then they are ready to be manipulated. A society of people under the evil spell and enchantment of behaviorism is ready to be controlled. We must resist such techniques of manipulation at all levels. We must teach our children to reason rather than to simply respond mindlessly to socially engineered stimuli.

IN AS MUCH AS *the secular world view is based upon the view that man is a machine or an animal; and,*
FURTHERMORE *since those adhering to the secular behavioral view are in areas of great influence within our country seeking to control and manipulate our children;*

THEREFORE, LET US HIGHLY RESOLVE

to provide every opportunity to foster the reasoning abilities of our children so that they will be able to discern the thoughts and ideas implicit in major statements made through art, music, literature, science, or government; so that our children will be able to recognize what is not being said as well as what is spoken — in order to understand not simply what is written but what is written between the lines.

Resolve Number Four

TO ENTER INTO TRUE SPIRITUALITY

"I have come that you might have life and have it more abundantly."
— John 10:10

The great difference between present-day Christianity and that of which we read in these letters [the New Testament Epistles] is that to us it is primarily a performance; to them it was a real experience. We are apt to reduce the Christian religion to a code, or at best a rule of heart and life. To these men it is quite plainly the invasion of their lives by a new quality of life altogether. They do not hesitate to describe this as Christ "living in" them.[1]

— J.B. Phillips

People may be able to speak on the doctrine of co-death without knowing the power of this death. Or to converse on resurrection life without experiencing its power. If all we talk about is doctrine, we are handling something dead.... We need to learn the lesson of knowing life. For life depends not on how enthusiastic is our emotion or on how manifold is our thought; it rests exclusively on whether the Lord has manifested His own self. There is therefore nothing more important than to know the Lord.[2]

— Watchman Nee

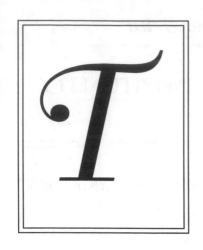

Twentieth century man continues to search for fulfillment. Three choices, three roads, three maps, are available to him. 1) Man moves beyond freedom and dignity as he is conditioned and programmed into a higher form of animal; 2) Man reaches to a higher state of consciousness through contact with the impersonal Force of the New Age; 3) Man returns to his proper relationship with the Creator and finds true spirituality as explained from the Biblical world view.

The map of humanism leads to a loss of the true humanness of man. The map of the New Age directs man toward a false spirituality. The Biblical world view leads to the personal-infinite God. Only as man bows to God as both Creator and Savior will he find ultimate fulfillment.

In an effort to maintain doctrinal purity, Christians have the tendency to slip into acting as if Christianity were simply a code of ethics to live by. Although Christianity provides an absolute moral gauge against which we can measure society and our personal lives, it is so much more. We must guard against a twentieth century sterilization in which we separate the content of Christianity from the life and power of Christ. Christianity must not be reduced to simply

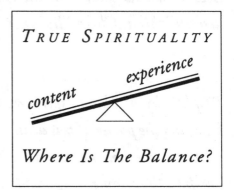

a system of beliefs, a philosophy, or a code of ethics. Some segments within Christianity emphasize doctrine while others emphasize experience. What is the proper balance? What is true spiritual reality?

Instead of starting with a definition, we will let three people describe the reality of Christ in their own life.

Examples of True Spiritual Reality

Francis Schaeffer on True Spirituality
from his book *Two Contents, Two Realities* [3]

"Back in 1951 and 1952, I went through a very deep time in my own life. I had been a pastor for ten years and a missionary for another five, and I was connected with a group who stood very strongly for the truth of the Scriptures. But as I watched, it became clear to me that I saw very little spiritual reality. I had to ask why. I looked at myself as well and realized that my own spiritual reality was not as great as it had been immediately after my conversion. We were in Switzerland at the time, and I said to my wife, 'I must really think this through.'

"I took about two months, and I walked in the mountains whenever it was clear. And when it was rainy, I walked back and forth in the hayloft over our chalet. I thought and wrestled and prayed, and I went all the way back to my agnosticism. I asked myself whether I had been right to stop being an agnostic and to become a Christian. I told my wife, if it didn't turn out right I was going to be honest and go back to America and put it all aside and do some other work.

"I came to realize that indeed I had been right in becoming a Christian. But then I went on further and wrestled deeper and asked, "But then where is the spiritual reality, Lord, among most of that which calls itself orthodoxy?" And gradually I found something. I found something that I had not been taught, a simple thing but profound. I discovered the meaning of the work of Christ, the meaning of the blood of Christ, moment by moment in our lives after we are Christians — the moment-by-moment work of the whole Trinity in our lives because as Christians we are indwelt by the Holy Spirit. That is true spirituality."

Hudson Taylor on The Exchanged Life
as reported by V. Raymond Edman in his book *They Found the Secret* [4]

"As to work, mine was never so plentiful, so responsible, or so difficult; but the weight and strain are all gone ... When my agony of soul was at its height ... the Spirit of God revealed the truth of our oneness with Jesus as I had never known it before. McCarthy, who had [experienced] the same sense of failure but saw the light before I did, wrote: 'But how to get faith strengthened? Not by striving after faith, but by resting on the Faithful One.'

"As I read I saw it all! 'If we believe not, He abideth faithful.' I looked to Jesus and saw that He had said, 'I will never leave you.' 'Ah, there is rest!' I thought. I have striven in vain to rest in Him. I'll strive no more. For has He not promised to abide with me — never to leave me, never to fail me?

"But this was not all He showed me, nor one half. As I thought of the Vine and branches, what light the blessed Spirit poured into my soul! How great seemed my mistake in having wished to get the sap, the fullness out of Him. I saw not only that Jesus would never leave me, but that I was a member of His body, of His flesh and of His bones. The vine now I see, is not the root merely, but all — root, stem, branches, twigs, leaves, flowers, fruit; and Jesus is not only that: He is soil and sunshine, air and showers and ten thousand times more than we have ever dreamed, wished for, or needed. Oh, the joy of seeing this truth! I do pray that the eyes of your understanding may be enlightened, that you may know and enjoy the riches freely given us in Christ.

"The sweetest part... is the rest which full identification with Christ brings. I am no longer anxious about anything, as I realize this; for He, I know, is able to carry out His will, and His will is mine."

Ian Thomas on Christ – My Life
from *They Found the Secret*[5] by V.R. Edman

"I was a windmill of activity, until, at the age of nineteen, every moment of my day was packed tight with doing things: preaching, talking, counselling. The only thing that alarmed me was that nobody was converted! That gets a little discouraging after a bit, doesn't it? The more I did, the less happened ... But I discovered that forever doubling and redoubling my efforts in order to win souls, rushing here and dashing there... did nothing, nothing, nothing to change the utter barrenness, the emptiness, the uselessness of my activity. I tried to make up with noise what I lacked in effectiveness and power.

"Then, one night in November, that year, just at midnight, in my room at home, I got down on my knees before God, and I just wept in sheer despair. I said, 'Oh, God, ...with all my heart I have wanted to serve Thee. I have tried to my uttermost and I am a hopeless failure! So far as doing anything more, I am finished.'

"God, that night, simply focused upon me the Bible message of Christ Who is our Life. This was the moment He had been waiting for; seven weary years He had watched me running round and round in the wilderness! He had been waiting for the time when at last I would fall down in hopeless despair. I heard His voice: 'to me to live is Christ.' Life! New Life! To me to live is Christ!

"It just came from every area of God's Word, and very kindly and very lovingly the Lord seemed to make it plain to me: 'You see, for seven years, with utmost sincerity, you have been trying to live *for* Me, on My behalf, the life that I have been waiting for seven years to live *through* you.'"

What is the Secret?

Jesus promised an "abundant life." Is that how you would describe the life of your Christian friends or even your own life? Why is it that so few Christians live this kind of life? Living the Christian life is not hard; it is actually impossible. Only one person has ever lived this life successfully and that was Jesus Himself. What was His secret? Did He live a perfect life because He is God? Actually, He lived this quality of life not because He was God (though He is), but rather He lived this life because He was man! This may come as some surprise to you. Let me explain. Jesus said "I assure you, most solemnly I tell you, the Son is able to do nothing from Himself — of His own accord ... I am able to do nothing from Myself — independently, of My own accord ... I have no desire to do what is pleasing to Myself, My own aim, My own purpose" (John 5:19, 30). So If Jesus didn't live the Christian life perfectly because He is the Second Person of the Trinity, then how was it lived? He was living, as the second Adam, in complete and total dependence upon the Father in the power of the Holy Spirit. His secret was not in His being God, but rather His living as man was intended to live - in absolute surrender to the Father. He was living as the first Adam was to live.

What insight does this shed upon our daily living as Christians? Just as Jesus said that He could do nothing apart from His Father, He told His disciples that "apart from Me you can do nothing" (John 15:5). This is the secret! He desires to go on today living his life moment-by-moment through Christians in whom He lives. This is true spirituality. You may ask: "How can I enter into this 'abundant life'?"

Awareness

Though the details differ for each person, there does appear to be a general pattern that emerges from the lives of Christians who have and are living in true spirituality. We say this cautiously because there is the tendency to turn things into simple formulas. Life and real spiritual reality can not be reduced to such a formula!

We know that the Christian life begins by accepting through faith the finished work of Christ. Paul explains that "much more then, being now justified by his blood, we shall be saved from wrath through Him" (Romans 5:9). At regeneration the Holy Spirit restores to us the very life of God that was lost when Adam and Eve believed the lie that they could be like God. The Apostle Peter writes that we are "partakers of the Divine Nature" (II Peter 1: 3). The very life of God, the resurrection life of Christ fills our lives as believers.

Unfortunately, we have reduced salvation to mean God getting us out of hell and into heaven. Not long after our regeneration, many of us return to our old life pattern based upon self-effort and self-determination. This return of course, results in defeat or denial in our personal lives (Matthew 9:36). 'I want to do what is right, but do not seem to be able to do so' becomes our life pattern (Romans 7:18-20,24). We try and fail. We try again, just a little harder, but we still fail. We are told we need greater commitment, greater dedication, greater involvement, or greater faith. This really means that we should try harder to be like Christ!

Imagine holding a partially inflated balloon in your hand. You want to squeeze it in order to conform it to your hand. As you do, you notice that the balloon begins to come out between two of your fingers. In an attempt to get control of that portion of the balloon, you push it in with a finger from the other hand. But as you do, the balloon pushes out at another location! Try as you might, the balloon keeps coming out. It is impossible to get total control of the balloon. When we try to conform our lives to the character of Christ, we fail. We may get control of one area of our life only to find that another area has pushed out.

"Christian character is not developed, or 'built' through human attention and energy," explains Lewis Sperry Chafer (founder of Dallas Theological Seminary). He goes on to further explain: "The method of attaining unto a character by attention and energy, which is now elaborately explained and constantly recommended by many, is the best the world can do, and that method may have some realization within the sphere of the shadows the world has chosen as its ideas. ...But true Christian character is the 'fruit of the Spirit.' ... It is no longer something for the human strength to attempt, nor is it to be done by the human strength plus the help of the spirit. It is not something that man can do, even with help. It is 'the fruit of the Spirit.' *True Christian character is produced in the believer, but not by the believer.*"

When we become aware of our inability to imitate the character of Christ, God has brought us to a crossroads in our Christian life. Our awareness of not being able to live the Christian life successfully leads us to either giving up any hope of living life differently and simply going into a holding pattern until heaven, or entering into true spirituality. The apostle Paul described his inner conflict as a "waging war against the law of [his] mind, and making [him] a prisoner of the law of sin which is in [his] members" (Romans 7: 23). Is it really possible that the man used by God to write so much of the New Testament would have this same difficulty? Paul goes on to describe himself: "Wretched man that I am! Who will set me free from the body of this death" (Romans 7:24)?

Do you have a sin pattern, an addiction of some kind, that seems to be reoccurring in your life that you have tried to overcome? Does it seem that it has attached itself to you like a parasite which you are unable to pull off? Have you ever asked like Paul, "How can I get free from this?" Yes, such spiritual struggle is reality, but it need not produce slavery. The answer to this question is the basic consideration of the Christian life. In *True Spirituality* Francis Schaeffer explains

> First, Christ died in history. Second, Christ rose in history. Third, we died with Christ in history, when we accepted Him as our Savior. Fourth, we will be raised in history when He comes again. Fifth, we are to live by faith now as though we were now dead, as though we have already died. And sixth, we are to live now by faith as though we have now already been raised from the dead.[6]

"Thanks be to God through Jesus Christ our Lord!" Paul explains. "So then, on the one hand I myself with my mind am serving the law of God, but on the other, with my flesh the law of sin. There is therefore now no condemnation for those who are in Christ Jesus. For the law of the Spirit of life in Christ Jesus has set you free from the law of sin and of death" (Romans 7:25-8:1, 2). Our salvation is three fold. First, we are saved from the *penalty* of sin through the substitutionary death of Christ. Second, we will be saved from the *presence* of sin at His return. But what happens between these two points in time? Third, we are saved from the *power* of sin in this life by our identification with the resurrected Christ.

The beauty of the Christian world view is that we know the source of conflict. We do not have to imagine the conflict away or cover it up through drugs or work or some form of denial. Neither do we have to blame our parents or our childhood environment. It goes all the way back to Genesis 3 and the literal, historic fall of man. At that moment in history man became separated from God. Much like a series of dominoes toppling, this event resulted in a series of other separations: mankind became separated from other men; individually man became separated from himself; husband and wife became separated from each other; mankind became separated from nature; and nature became separated from itself.

Picasso and other artists have often pictured man in this state of separation. The fragmented figures of Picasso reflect this abnormality. Unfortunately, such artists not realizing or rejecting that this world is abnormal create on canvas a hopeless, meaningless, and fragmented world. In order for man to find his true identity and then to be able to apply appropriate solutions to these problems, he must return to God's revealed truth about his beginnings. We must stand strongly on the truth of Scripture (particularly the first eleven chapters of Genesis) and be willing to give honest answers to honest questions.

Abandonment

There is a piece of music that has come to mean a lot to our family. It is beloved by believers because it contains the melody for a wonderful hymn; however, the composer was describing the struggle between two nations. Finland was under the dominance of Russia at the time, and Jean Sibelius, the composer, dramatically portrayed this conflict in this composition *Finlandia*.[7] Because of the affect this music had on the people of Finland, the Russian government forbade it to be played. Nevertheless, it was played in a variety of cities under a variety of names.

The first part of the piece involves great conflict and tension with short glimmers of hope. The conflict of the first part is set adjacent to the peace and tranquility of the second. It is at this point we begin singing in our minds:

> Be still my soul! the Lord is on thy side; Bear patiently the cross of grief or pain; Leave to thy God to order and provide; In every change He faithful will remain. Be still, my soul! thy best, thy heavenly Friend Through thorny ways leads to a joyful end.[8]

Yes, we know *Finlandia* as *Be Still My Soul*. Unfortunately for us as Christians, we are not aware of the first part of the music. We must never forget that true spirituality many times comes out of a life of conflict as we resolve to abandon our lives to God. Paul writes that in light of all that God has done for us through Christ that we are to resolutely 'present [our] bodies a living and holy sacrifice, acceptable to God, which is [our] spiritual service of worship. And do not be conformed to this world, but be transformed by the renewing of your mind, that you may prove what the will of God is, that which is good and acceptable and perfect (Romans 12:1,2). We are not robots pre-programmed by God. He is lovingly pursuing and drawing us to Himself—waiting for us to abandon ourselves to Him.

Listen to the complete work of *Finlandia* by Sibelius and remember that we can only "Be Still" while the inner war is waging if we resolutely abandon and present our lives to God.

Availability

Does it end here? No, this is only the beginning of true spiritual reality. There are two phrases that must become as natural to us as breathing:

> • Every command of Scripture is a promise.
> • Whatever God requires He performs.

Although we can not keep the commandments of God in our own strength, "it is God Who is all the while effectually at work in you, —

energizing and creating in you the power and desire — both **to will** and **to work** for His good pleasure and satisfaction and delight" (Philippians 2:13). We can have confidence that "if we ask anything according to His will, He hears us. And if we know that He hears us in whatever we ask, we know that we have the requests which we have asked from Him" (I John 5:14, 15).

Jesus said the Kingdom of God was near and the Kingdom of God was within you (Luke 10:9; 17:21). Jesus desires to be King in His Kingdom - in our hearts. Make yourself available to Him so that He can rule in your life moment-by-moment. He is at work in you to live His life through you.

Abiding

Is this simply a once and for all decision? Not at all. Christ ruling in our lives must be a moment-by-moment reality. Jesus describes this life in the illustration of the branch and the vine (John 15: 1-17). Andrew Murray in his book *Absolute Surrender* [9] describes this abiding life:

— A Life of Absolute *Dependence* —

"The branch has nothing; it just depends upon the vine for everything. If I can learn every moment of the day to depend upon God, everything will come right. You will get the higher life if you depend absolutely upon God. Here we find it with the vine and the branches. Every vine you ever see, or every bunch of grapes that comes upon your table, let it remind you that the branch is absolutely dependent on the vine. The vine has got to do the work, and the branch enjoys the fruit of it.

— A Life of *Deep Restfulness* —

"Oh that little branch, if it could think and if it could feel, and if it could speak - if we could have a little branch here today to talk to us, and if we could say, 'Come, branch of the vine, tell me, I want to learn from thee how I can be a true branch of the living Vine,' what would it answer: The little branch would whisper: 'Man, I hear that you're wise, and I know that you can do a great many wonderful things. I know you have much strength and wisdom given to you, but I have one lesson for you. With all your hurry and effort in Christ's work you never prosper. The first thing you need is to come and rest in your Lord Jesus. That is what I do. Since I grew out of that vine I have just to rest in the vine. When the time of spring came I had no anxious thought or care. The vine began to pour its sap into me, and to give the bud and leaf. And when the time of summer came I had no care, and in the great heat I trusted the vine to bring moisture to keep me fresh. And in the time of harvest, when the owner came to pluck the grapes, I had no care. And if you would be a true branch of the living Vine just rest on Him. Let Christ bear the responsibility.'... Come and understand that it is the Lord Jesus who wants to work through you."

— A Life of *Much Fruitfulness* —

"You know the Lord Jesus repeated that word fruit often in the parable. He spoke, first, of fruit, and then of more fruit, and then of much fruit. Yes, you are ordained not only to bear fruit, but to bear much fruit. 'Herein is My Father glorified, that you bear much fruit.' In the first place, Christ said, 'I am the Vine, and My Father is the Husbandman.' My Father is the Husbandman who has charge of Me and you. He who will watch over the connection between Christ and the branches is God; and it is in the power of God through Christ we are to bear fruit."

— A Life of *Resolute Surrender* —

"Oh, friends, we want this entire surrender to the Lord Jesus Christ. What is this entire surrender ... It means that just as literally as Christ was given up entirely to God, I am given up entirely to Christ ... Our relation to Jesus ought to be such that we are entirely at His disposal, and every day come to Him humbly and straightforwardly and say: Lord, is there anything in me that is not according to Thy will, that has not been ordered by Thee, or that is not entirely given up to Thee?"

"Oh, let it be a prayer from the depths of our heart, that the living Christ may take each one of us and link us close to Himself. Let our prayer be that He, the living Vine, shall so link each of us to Himself that we shall go away with our hearts singing: He is my Vine, and I am His branch, — I want nothing more, — now I have the everlasting Vine. Then, when you get alone with Him, worship and adore Him, praise and trust Him, love Him and wait for His love. Thou art my Vine, and I am Thy branch."

Abundance

Jesus described the Christian life as an "abundant life" (John 10:10). What is this *abundant life* promised by Jesus? V. Raymond Edman described it with these words: "It is new life for old. It is rejoicing for weariness and radiance for dreariness. It is strength for weakness, and steadiness for uncertainty. It is triumph even through tears, and tenderness of heart instead of touchiness."[10] The apostle Paul described this life when he said, "I am crucified with Christ: nevertheless I live; yet not I, but Christ lives in me: and the life which I now live in the flesh I live by the faith of the Son of God, who loved me, and gave Himself for me" (Galatians 2:20). True spirituality is the life of Christ lived moment-by-moment.

The Role of World Views

According to Pascal, the great French physicist, there exists a "vacuum in the heart of man."[11] Man is attempting to fill this void within himself. Man is seeking spirituality. We have said that a world view is a map. Ultimately we must know where the map is leading us. The world view actually leads man to know how and with what to fill this void. The vacuum within man must be filled. He cannot continue to live with this void. Depending upon the world view held to be true, man will find either true spirituality or false spirituality. Therefore, world view questions are not simply an academic exercise for our mind, but rather they actually lead man to ultimate reality.

The naturalistic world view is in difficulty at this point. Man may be unique, but so are whales. If taken to its logical conclusion, naturalism leaves man with nothing to fill the void. He then turns to drugs, popular music, materialism, or a host of other possibilities. Of course, these are mere anesthetics to numb the pain of emptiness. Naturalism, if taken seriously, leads to Nihilism, the loss of meaning altogether. Man is plummeted into a personal cosmic black hole - moving faster and faster toward nothingness. Hemingway, in his book *Old Man and the Sea,*[12] accurately portrays the meaninglessness of existence and resulting despair. Man at this point only has a limited number of choices.

Suicide is one way out. However, man is pinned into reality by God. Unlike the plant or animal kingdoms, man has a natural fear of death. Therefore, suicide is not an attractive option for most people.

In an attempt to escape this dilemma, twentieth century man seeks "self-actualization" or a "higher consciousness". Both are false spiritualities. They are imitations, only shadows of what is real.

Returning to the thought of Pascal, he said that this vacuum is a "God-shaped vacuum in the heart of every man which only God can fill through His Son, Jesus Christ."[13] Only the Biblical world view will direct and lead man into true spirituality.

The Biblical world view starts with God. This may sound too simple, but it is profound. The God of the Bible is unlike the impersonal gods of the East and unlike the finite gods of Greece and Rome. He is both infinite and personal. This is not an order. He is not first infinite and then personal, but rather he is both infinite and personal.

Who am I? Man is unique from the rest of the living and nonliving world. Other world views may include a similar statement, but only the Biblical world view gives an adequate explanation for this uniqueness. Man was created in the image of God. *Where am I from?* Again this world view question points man back to the Creator-creature relationship. It points man back to the infinite and personal God. Man is the direct creation of God. *Where am I going?* is a question of eternal destiny. The Biblical world view is not a philosophy or an empty orthodoxy, but rather true spirituality. The early Christians understood this to be "Christ living in" them.

An Illustration

During the early 1970's a person shared this illustration with us. It was a time line of a person's life. This diagram, though far from complete, charts the pattern. Keep in mind that the circumstances surrounding each person's life will be different, but the decisions to move toward true spirituality may be similar.

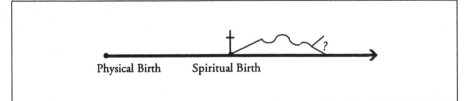

I was born into the family of Quines in 1949. I was born into the family of God in 1967. For a time I grew in my understanding of Christ. Then my life began to level off or even to drop back down. There were many ups and downs. Life was like a roller coaster. I tried to be like Christ by trying to imitate His life. However, I only found frustration and failure. Then God brought me to a decision of returning to a mere existence or entering into true spiritual reality. This was the beginning of my moment-by-moment experience of Christ's resurrection life through my life.

Where are you in your personal walk with Christ? Draw a time-line of your own life and then share the details with your family.

IN AS MUCH AS *Christianity is more than a philosophy of life or a code of ethics to live by; and,*
FURTHERMORE, *since true spirituality can only be found in the moment-by-moment work of Christ in my life;*

THEREFORE, LET US HIGHLY RESOLVE

to enter into true spirituality and find ultimate fulfillment, purpose, and meaning to life through our identification with Christ and the power of His resurrection through His Holy Spirit.

To Be 'By Faith' Families

"While we look not at the things which are seen, but at the things which are not seen; for the things which are seen are temporal, but the things which are not seen are eternal. We walk by faith, not sight."

—*Colossians 3:12-14*

Household of Faith
Here we are at the start committing to each other
By His word and from our hearts
We will be a family in a house that will be a home
And with faith we'll build it strong.

Now to be a family, we've got to love each other
At any cost unselfishly
And our home must be a place that fully abounds with grace
A reflection of His face.

We'll build a household of faith
That together we can make
And when the strong winds blow it won't fall down
As one in Him we'll grow and the whole world will know
That we are a household of faith. [1]

— Brent Lamb & John Rosasco

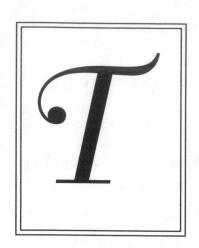here is an amazing phenomena spreading across our land today. It is spreading like a cancer. We are referring to the lottery. Think about it for a moment. Against all reason, against staggering odds, and against all logic, billions of dollars are being spent annually by people who *hope* they will win the jackpot. Mathematically such hope is illogical; it is irrational! This type of faith results from a people who are not reasoning. The Disney classic expressed it so well: *When you wish upon a star....Like a bolt out of the blue, fate steps in to see you through...and all your dreams come true.*[2]

Is this an example of Biblical faith? Certainly not. Biblical faith is not a hope in hope nor a crossing of fingers and hoping for the best. Neither is it a knocking on wood. It is not a desperate, blind leap into the dark.

We hear "Good Luck!" falling from the lips of believer and unbeliever alike. Because we are surrounded with such a pervasive false view of hope and faith, it is imperative that we have a proper understanding of true Biblical faith. Biblical faith is "the assurance of things hoped for and the convictions of things not yet seen" (Hebrews 11:1). Assurance is the state of being certain and confident. Conviction is the strong persuasion or belief. It is the state of being convinced. It denotes certainty. Because Biblical Christianity is set

> **ASSURANCE**
> *the state of being certain and confident.*
>
> **CONVICTION**
> *the strong persuasion or belief. It is the state of being convinced. It denotes certainty.*

into the concrete remembrances in history of the faithfulness of the infinite-personal God, our hope and faith is very different from that of many 20th century ideas. God has spoken to us in propositional truth in history, and He expects us to respond appropriately by faith.

Living by faith in a day and age that denies the spiritual dimension of history makes decisions based upon the eternal perspective seem irrational and therefore illogical. There was a time in Western culture that such decisions were compatible with Christianity; however living in a "post-Christian" cultural consensus, *by faith families* are living outside the acceptable norm. Being "by faith families'" most likely will mean that we are at times politically incorrect. From a human perspective we must be prepared to walk by ourselves. This takes the courage, *the resolve,* of a Daniel. The Bible provides an adequate framework for being a household of faith.

From Faith to Faith

Abraham, Isaac, Jacob, and Joseph form a continuity of faith that stands as a model for us today. They represent four generations who walked with God. All four generations are included in God's Hall of Faith (Hebrews 11). Perfect? Far from it. Pleasing to God? Most definitely. What one characteristic did these men have in common? "Living by faith" — for "without faith it is impossible to please [God]" (Hebrews 11: 6). If we continue reading in Hebrews, we learn that:

• *By Faith* Abraham left his homeland to live in a foreign land looking for a holy city whose architect and builder is God....

• *By Faith* Isaac blessed Jacob and Esau...

• *By Faith* Jacob blessed each of Joseph's sons and worshipped God....

• *By Faith* Joseph spoke of the future reality of God delivering His people.

In Psalms 78 verses 5 -7 we read:

> For He established a testimony in Jacob, and appointed a law in Israel, which He commanded our fathers, that they should teach them to their children, that the generation to come might know, even the children yet to be born, that they may arise and tell them to their children, that they should put their confidence in God, and not forget the works of God, but keep His commandments.

The Psalmist speaks of four generations — from faith to faith. What was to be transferred from father to son, from son to grandson, from grandson to great grandson? A confidence in God. What kind of confidence? That God is and that He is the rewarder of those who seek Him. The question is not how large our faith is, but rather, how large our God is! We are to be passing on to each succeeding generation our personal knowledge and love of the infinite-personal God. How is this possible?

Each older generation was to "teach and tell" so the coming generation "might know." This was not to be a blind obedience to cold theoretical theology, but rather a personal knowledge of the life and power of God in their own lives. And what was to be the result? Obedience. They were to realize that walking by faith in obedience to all that He had instructed yielded a life of spiritual abundance. If we reduce Christianity to merely a code of ethics, rules to be lived by, and omit the personal walk with God, we miss the mark. However, if we know God but ignore His commands, we do not really love Him (John 14:21).

Continuity of faith from one generation to the next builds households of faith. As in days of old, today's families profoundly impact their children, grandchildren and great-grandchildren. You may find your family, like Abraham, just beginning the procession of faith, or perhaps you are in the process of passing your faith from the previous generation to the next. Edith Schaeffer compares a family to a relay race [3] in which the baton of truth is passed from one generation to the next. If the baton of your family heritage has been dropped, pick it up and run with the speed of the wind. If you are the second or third leg in this *by faith* continuity, then make sure that you securely carry it on to the next generation. Let us resolve to pass the life of faith from our generation to the next with a crisp, clean transfer to our children.

The apostle Paul writes, "the things which you have heard from me in the presence of many witnesses, these entrust to faithful men, who will be able to teach others also" (II Timothy 2:2). Does this sound similar to the passage from the Psalms? What is the progression? Paul is speaking of four generations — Paul to Timothy, Timothy to faithful men, and faithful men to others — from faith to faith. Discipleship is reaching people in our unique sphere of influence. Is there a more unique sphere than our children and grandchildren? *There is no greater calling than making disciples, and there is no greater opportunity than discipling our children.*

Spiritual continuity from generation to generation allows us to build and pass on the spiritual heritage of who God is and what He has done for us personally. Just as Joseph could reflect back four generations to his forefather Abraham to see God's personal faithfulness to his own family, so can we build a household of faith for the next generation. In the future we do not want it said about our children's generation "there arose another generation who did not know the Lord, nor the work which He had done for us" (Judges 2:10).

Living in Light of the Unexpected

God provides unexpected events and circumstances to make us *by faith families*. When Abraham and Sarah were old and the promised child had not yet been born, did this barren couple expect Sarah would conceive and bear a child? When Moses led the Israelites from Egypt and they became trapped with the Red Sea in front and the Egyptian army behind, did Moses expect the sea to part to allow them to pass through? When the disciples told Jesus to send away the 5,000 so that they could find food and lodging, did they expect Jesus to say *you feed them*? What was the most unexpected event in history? Though the prophets had foretold it, the Pharisees did not expect it, and the Sadducees had rejected it. The Romans laughed at it. Even the disciples did not believe it! Yet, the resurrection of Jesus changed the course of history.

God uses unexpected events to confirm to us that He is who He is and that He is the rewarder of those who seek Him. When there is a mismatch between what we expect and what God does, He is then teaching us to be *by faith families*. He is redrawing our map, our world view.

In the children's classic series *Narnia*, Aslan, a type of Christ, is referred to as "no tame lion." What was C. S. Lewis conveying? We cannot put God in a mold or box. God is much larger than our thoughts, and His actions are beyond our comprehension. Living in light of the unexpected will make us *by faith families*.

Concrete Remembrances

We read in Joshua 4: 1-9:

> Now it came about when all the nation had finished crossing the Jordan, that the LORD spoke to Joshua, saying,

"Take for yourselves twelve men from the people, one man from each tribe, and command them, saying, 'Take up for yourselves twelve stones from here out of the middle of the Jordan, from the place where the priests' feet are standing firm, and carry them over with you, and lay them down in the lodging place where you will lodge tonight.'"

So Joshua called the twelve men whom he had appointed from the sons of Israel, one man from each tribe; and Joshua said to them, "Cross again to the ark of the LORD your God into the middle of the Jordan, and each of you take up a stone on his shoulder, according to the number of the tribes of the sons of Israel. Let this be a sign among you, so that when your children ask later, saying, 'What do these stones mean to you?' then you shall say to them, 'Because the waters of the Jordan were cut off before the ark of the covenant of the LORD; when it crossed the Jordan, the waters of the Jordan were cut off.' So these stones shall become a memorial to the sons of Israel forever."

And thus the sons of Israel did, as Joshua commanded, and took up twelve stones from the middle of the Jordan, just as the LORD spoke to Joshua, according to the number of the tribes of the sons of Israel; and they carried them over with them to the lodging place, and put them down there.

Then Joshua set up twelve stones in the middle of the Jordan at the place where the feet of the priests who carried the ark of the covenant were standing, and they are there to this day.

As families traveled through this area of the Jordan River, young Jewish children would naturally ask, "Mommie and Daddy, how did those stones get into the middle of the river?" This question would naturally lead into a discussion of the reality of God and His work in their personal lives. Such concrete remembrances are one way in which God transfers truth from one generation to the next. It was expected that within the family the personal knowledge of God would pass. Throughout history several sign posts or large billboards have served to evoke discussions concerning faith so that the next generation can know the personal-infinite God of Heaven. Through these evidences of God's working, each generation is spurred on to trust the Lord in their lives. God has given us other memorials, established by Him as concrete remembrances. These include feasts, readings, the Sabbath, and even the rainbow.

We were a young couple with two small children. I was a teacher and Shirley was staying home with our children. We were renting a tiny two bedroom duplex. The news came that we were expecting. But not just expecting. We were expecting a double blessing — TWINS! Was it possible? A myriad of thoughts and feelings flooded our minds. How could we make it? In the past we had searched for a larger place to live, but at our salary level there was nothing else in reach. Would we push the panic button? God was at work in us to strengthen our "shaky" faith. What would God do, if anything? Would we trust Him and give thanks no matter what the outcome?

One year later when the twins were seven months old just as it looked like we were going to have to give up our bedroom to have a place for the twins to sleep, God did the unexpected. I was given a promotion that only two months earlier I was told I was not qualified to fill. God orchestrated the circumstances to provide for our needs in a most unexpected way. As we drive by that little duplex on Custer Road, it serves as a concrete remembrance to our family that God will faithfully provide for our changing needs.

Today, *by faith families* should erect such sign posts for their children and grandchildren. These natural opportunities will teach our children and our children's children of God's past faithfulness in our personal lives which will in turn serve as a base for them to trust the Lord in their lives. This continuity from one generation to the next will encourage our children to live by faith, not by sight.

Living by Faith — Not by Sight

There are times in our life when there is confusion. There is a temporary detour on our map. At least it looks like a detour to us. It is at these times we must not rely on our instincts, but carefully get through the confusion by closely following and relying upon the directions. This principle is illustrated when driving through the Dallas-Fort Worth

Airport. While exiting the terminal every local person knows south is to the left. However, the sign directs the driver to the right. A conflict in a person's mind begins between feelings and reason. While reason says follow the sign, emotions try to redirect the driver in the opposite way. Do feelings or emotions rule? I often believe the sign is wrong. Shirley is more likely to follow the sign. The result: I get lost! The moral is: Don't rely upon your feelings when driving around airports or through life.

In life there will be confusion, apparent detours. Such discomfiture is very real. If we deny reality, we do not benefit our situation. God is taking us by a way which at the moment we do not understand, and it is only by going through the confusion that He will make us *by faith families*.

Oswald Chambers, in *My Utmost for His Highest*, explains that

> "Jesus gave the illustration of the man who looked as if he did not care for his friend, and He said that that is how the Heavenly Father will appear to you at times. You will think He is an unkind friend, but remember He is not; the times will come when everything will be explained. There is a cloud on the friendship of the heart, and often even love itself has to wait in pain and tears for the blessing of fuller communion. When God looks completely shrouded, will you hang on in confidence in Him?
>
> "Jesus says there are times when your Father will appear as if He were an unnatural father, as if He were callous and indifferent, but remember He is not; I have told you — 'Everyone that asketh receiveth,' If there is a shadow on the face of the Father just now, hang onto it that He will ultimately give His clear revealing and justify Himself in all that He permitted (Luke 11).
>
> "'When the Son of Man cometh, shall He find faith on the earth?' Will He find the faith which banks on Him in spite of the confusion? Stand off in faith believing that what Jesus said is true, though in the meantime you do not understand what God is doing. He has bigger issues at stake than the particular things you ask" (Luke 18:1-8).[4]

IN AS MUCH AS *the current cultural definition of faith rests upon chance and a hope that stands against statistical odds; and,* FURTHERMORE, *since true Biblical faith rests upon the character of the infinite-personal God,*

THEREFORE, LET US HIGHLY RESOLVE

to be by faith families *even when our thoughts and ideas, our actions and attitudes, while being congruent with the Biblical world view demand that we cross the consensus of our culture. May God grant us the wisdom, the convictions, and the* resolve *to make such decisions, that our faith may pass from generation to generation.*

A Personal Addendum - *from faith to faith ...*

Our eldest son, hoping and praying, to be able to attend a small private college, had patiently taken classes at a nearby community college. He questioned how God would provide to meet his need. After applying at a particular college he learned that he was the recipient of a very nice scholarship. A new billboard had been erected in his mind, indicating God's infinite and personal care for him.

Our second son was in need of a better piano, for he was soon to be having auditions with several music conservatories. We prayed and looked for a quality piano, but they were all too expensive. In the face of this confusion our son could have given up playing the piano or he could continued to trust God. He was at a faith barrier. A year later we received a telephone call from a lady whom we had never met. She had heard of our need and was offering us the use of her concert grand piano. As the piano movers brought in that beautiful black grand piano, we asked the movers if they believed in miracles. A 1000 pound billboard was erected and tucked into our young son's heart and mind.

Resolve Number Six

To Prepare Our Children as a 'Letter of Christ' to the Culture

"You are our letter, written in our hearts, known and read by all men; being manifested that you are a letter of Christ, cared for by us, written not with ink, but with the Spirit of the living God, not on tablets of stone, but on tablets of human hearts."

— 2 Corinthians 3: 2-3

It is important for Christians to pay close attention to the course of events. We are going to be called upon to answer questions we have never considered before, and we should be prepared to respond. First, we need to understand from the Christian world view what is happening. More important, we must help those in decision-making capacities to recognize the implications of the issues we face together as the human race. In short, Christians should prepare to take the lead in giving direction to cultural change. And if it goes poorly, as well it might in the post-Christian world, then we should be consciously preparing the next generation for the new battles it will face.[1]

— Francis Schaeffer

s we move closer to the twenty-first century, how can we meet the challenge of raising children to face these new battles. Dare we leave this preparation to chance? In contrast to chance, Dr. Schaeffer says that we must be making a conscious effort to establish the next generation — that is, *our children* — so that they will be ready to face the difficult days and decisions that lie ahead. Where can we gain perspective amidst the changing philosophical views?

The Letter

"You are our letter," explains the apostle Paul, "written in our hearts, known and read by all men; being manifested that you are a letter of Christ, cared for by us, written not with ink, but with the Spirit of the living God, not on tablets of stone, but on tablets of human hearts" (II Corinthians 3:2-3). Of course, Paul was writing to those whom he had discipled at Corinth; but, in essence, our children are becoming "our letter of Christ" as we care for them, and as they grow, they too will be "read by all men." What an eternal perspective. Pray that our children will have

> David and Shirley Quine
> 2006 Flat Creek
> Richardson, Texas
>
> 21st Century
>
> TO: Richardson
> Dallas
> Texas
> USA
> the World

soft hearts toward Christ and that they will become a clearly readable "letter of Christ" to a culture that so desperately needs to know Him. God has given us this wonderful opportunity. As we become *'by faith families'* we become like lights set on a hill. Our children will be able to offer the next generation the true map which directs society back to the personal-infinite God. The family is the first place discipleship should be happening.

Care for the Letter

Paul described his care for "the letter," those people whom he was discipling, with the analogy of a mother and father caring for their children:

> But we proved to be gentle among you, as a nursing *mother* tenderly cares for her own children. Having thus a fond affection for you, we were well-pleased to impart to you not only the gospel of God but also our own lives, because you had become very dear to us. For you recall, brethren, our labor and hardship, how working night and day so as not to be a burden to any of you, we proclaimed to you the gospel of God. You are witnesses, and so is God, how devoutly and uprightly and blamelessly we behaved toward you believers; just as you know how we were exhorting and encouraging and imploring each one of you as a *father* would his own children, so that you may walk in a manner worthy of the God who calls you into His own kingdom and glory (I Thessalonians 2: 7-12, emphasis added).

Paul used the example of a mother and father to describe discipleship —his "care of the letter." His first picture is that of a nursing mother gently and tenderly caressing and cherishing her child. Just as she imparts her whole life to this child, so does Paul to those whom he is discipling. I am reminded of Shirley waking in the middle of the night to care for the needs of our young children and then awake early the next morning to continue in her care. Yes, it was labor and hardship. It was "night and day."

Paul then enlarges the analogy to include the father. He explains that a father is given the role of exhorting each of his children personally. We are to be stimulating and encouraging them. A father is to give his children the vision and the direction to live their lives in such a way that his children reflect the character and nature of God. True discipleship means caring for the "letter of Christ that will be read by all men."

Writing the Letter

But, fathers must be careful. As fathers we are specifically instructed not to exasperate our children (Colossians 3:21). To exasperate is to embitter, to irritate, or to provoke. To exasperate our children will smudge the letter that is being written. We have been given the opportunity to partner with God in the writing of the letter. How should we approach the awesome responsibility of writing the letter of Christ to the culture?

The follow six principles are offered as guidelines. The word VIRTUE forms the basis of these ideas.

> V — Value our Children
> I — Inspire our Children
> R — Relate to our Children
> T — Teach our Children
> U — Unique, our Children are
> E — Example to our Children

Value Our Children!

What is the current cultural view of children? The worth of a person is often determined by his productivity: Person X Productivity = Worth. Think for a moment about young children. What do they produce? Usually, A MESS! In this formula *a mess* would be a negative number. Therefore, they would actually have a negative worth. Following this reasoning young children would not be considered an asset but rather a liability. How does this view of children compare with the Biblical view?

According to Solomon, "children are a gift of the LORD; the fruit of the womb is a reward. Like arrows in the hand of a warrior. How blessed is the man whose quiver is full of them..." (Psalm 127:3-5). What words are used to describe children? GIFT ... FRUIT ... REWARD. How is the father with children viewed? BLESSED! In the next Psalm we read: "How blessed is everyone who fears the LORD; Who walks in His ways. When you shall eat of the fruit of your hands, You will be happy and it will be well with you. Your wife shall be like a fruitful vine within your house. Your children like olive plants around your table. Behold, for thus shall the man be blessed who fears the LORD" (Psalm 128:1-4).

What word picture does the Psalmist give regarding children? Although it may sound strange to us to picture little olive plants around our dinner table, to a person from that region of the world at that time in history it was not. In fact, the olive plant was one of the most valuable trees of the ancient Hebrews. The olive tree was a symbol of beauty, strength, divine blessing, and prosperity. So, the next time one of those little olive plants knocks over a half gallon of milk at the breakfast table, REMEMBER! *they are a divine blessing! Tenderly care for these precious plants.*

Discipling a person takes time. Discipling an adult has value, but what about children? Have you ever had such a thought? Or maybe it never even crossed your mind that you should be discipling them. See how easy it is to have the attitude of the secular world infiltrate our own personal thinking about children? What is likely to happen if we fathers continue to ignore the command not to provoke our children to anger? Paul explains that they will "lose heart" (Colossians 3:21). To lose heart is to become frustrated or discouraged to the point of giving up. Paul says that if we do not watch out, our children will give up. They may turn from all that we hope and pray. How should we approach discipling our children?

As we work with them, we should have the same attitude Paul had toward those whom he was discipling: "For who is our hope and joy or crown of exultation? Is it not even you, in the presence of our Lord Jesus at His coming? For you are our glory and joy" (I Thessalonians 2:19-20). The word exult means to jump for joy! We should be jumping for joy for the opportunity to disciple our children. They will be "our glory and joy" at His coming! Because we value them, we will want to spend time with them giving to them the reality of knowing and loving God.

Inspire them!

We want to inspire them to know and love God. The primary way we get to know God is through the Bible. If we really believe that knowing God and His Son is the most vital experience in the world, dare we leave the responsibility for this instruction to someone else?

The best way to pass on a knowledge and love of God is through daily Bible reading and "singing and making melody" (Ephesians 5: 19) as a family. The most successful tool we have found for doing this is the *One Year Bible*. It made it "excuse-proof" in many ways since it provides short passages from both the Old or New Testament for every day. If we missed a day or even a couple of days we always knew exactly where to pick up next.

As we read, everyone present for the reading time was to think of a question they had about the passage. At first the questions were simple, but as the children grew and their spiritual understanding deepened so did their questions. It was exciting to see our children carefully thinking as they listened to the reading of God's Word. We could see that their understanding was deepening by the questions which they raised. As we were reading John chapter 4 these are some of the questions raised:

"Wasn't the woman lying when she said she had no husband?"
"What does it mean 'the fields are white for harvest'?"
"Why were the disciples surprised to learn that Jesus was talking with the Samaritan woman?"
"How did the woman's view of Jesus change?"
"How do we worship God?"

We found this approach to reading caused more careful listening and true thinking about the passage. God and His word became more meaningful to them.

In addition to the Bible, we want to inspire our children to develop virtuous character through reading together. How wonderful it would be to have a host of wise and godly friends to share their character with your children. According to Gladys Hunt in her book *Honey for a Child's Heart*:

> Books are like people:
>   fascinating, inspiring, thought-provoking,
> some laugh,
> some meditate,
>   others ache with old age, but still have wisdom;
> some are disease-ridden, some deceitful;
>   but others are a delight to behold,
> and many travel to foreign lands;
> some cry, some teach, others are lots of fun,
>   they are excellent companions,
> and all have individuality —
> Books are friends.
> What person has too many friends? [2]

What kind of books should we read together? A good book is always an experience containing spiritual, emotional, and intellectual dimensions. Charlotte Mason encourages us to lay before our children a feast of "living books." Ruth Sawyer describes these books as:

> Stories that make for wonder.
> Stories that make for laughter.
> Stories that stir one within with an understanding of the
> true nature of courage, of love, of beauty.
> Stories that make one tingle with high adventure,
>   with daring, with grim determination,
>   with the capacity of seeing danger through to the end.
> Stories that bring our minds to kneel in reverence;
> Stories that show the tenderness of true mercy,
>   the strength of loyalty,
>   the unmawkish respect for what is good.[3]

We also want to inspire them to love beautiful music and art. You may be asking yourself what music and art have to do with developing virtuous character: EVERYTHING!

> Whatever is true, whatever is worthy of reverence and is honorable and seemly, whatever is just, whatever is pure, whatever is lovely and lovable, whatever is kind and winsome and gracious, if there is any virtue and excellence, if there is anything worthy of praise, think on and weigh and take account of these things —fix your minds on them (Philippians 4: 8, Amplified Bible).

Artists and composers have always used their art forms to communicate their beliefs to the general culture. For example, Bach often wrote on his manuscripts, "With the help of Jesus" or "To God alone be the glory," acknowledging to all that his gift of music was from God. Even as it was true of Bach in his time, it is still true today. Such groups as *Mega Death* are using their music to communicate THEIR belief system to the children of our culture.

If you grew up like we did on a steady diet of "She loves you, Yea, Yea, Yea...."[4] you probably feel incapable of giving your children a love for beautiful music. The forward to *The Gift of Music* by Jane Stuart Smith and Betty Carlson offers this encouragement:

> Most of all, the purpose of this book is to encourage listening to the finest music with understanding and pleasure, and to stretch one's ears and imagination. The more we acquaint ourselves with that which is truly great and beautiful, the more we will dislike and turn away from that which is shallow and ugly. Also we want to show that what each artist believes in his heart and mind affects his creativity and those who follow him.[5]

Parents who read the Bible together with their children, who spend time developing a love for good literature and who learn to love beautiful music and art together, will have an unusual delight in what is good and true and an uncommon commitment to it. Spending this kind of quality time together will be deepening your relationship with your children.

Relate to Them!

Can you picture one person who loved you with an irresistible love — the kind of love which caused you to want to please them and to be like them? Were you fortunate enough to be given this kind of love by your mother, grandmother, father or grandfather? Many people we have talked with tell us there has not been even one person who caused them to feel deeply, unconditionally loved. But thank God, Jesus has loved us with such a deep transforming love, even if no one else ever has. He is our example of how to love and relate to our children.

Each of us wants to communicate this kind of unconditional love to his children, but most parents are not transmitting their own heartfelt love to their children. The reason is that they do not know how. Consequently, many children today do not feel genuinely, unconditionally loved and accepted.

The first way to communicate love to one's children is to love one's husband or wife. As husbands this means that we are to nourish and cherish our wives. As wives we are to defer to and admire our husbands. Modeling love to your children establishes security and stability for your family.

From the very beginning of his life a child longs for continuous, warm, consistent affection. How can we love our children so that they will cling to our values after they have left our shelter? We can ask God to give His gift of love because love cannot be produced by ourselves.

Unconditional love is conveyed through direct eye contact. Starting from those first hours when you hold your newborn in your arms and you bond. Softly speaking and staring into your child's eyes begins the communication process. Children can sense love for them when one looks directly into their eyes. Direct eye contact is a powerful way to communicate with anyone, but especially with one's children. You are saying, "I love you ... I am interested in what you have to say ... you are important ... I like to be with you ... You are of great value to me."

A word of caution! It can also be the means for sending many negative and disapproving messages. Use the eye gate carefully.

Another important communicator is physical contact. Touching another person says clearly "I love you; you are a worthwhile person." Physical and eye contact should be part of our everyday dealing with our children. It should be natural and comfortable, not showy or overdone. Special memories of eye contact and physical contact help strengthen young people so that they are able to stand against negative influences.

We are excited to tell you about another love communicator which has been very important to our family. Dr. Ross Campbell calls it focused attention.[6] It means giving our child our full undivided attention in such a way that he feels without a doubt that he is completely loved. This means of loving takes the magic ingredient T-I-M-E. Shirley and I started many years ago practicing what we call "Special Time." A few hours with one child alone, doing what he wants to do. Sometimes we went to a fast food restaurant for lunch, took a trip to the batting cages, went to the library, or just took a walk in the park together to feed the ducks. Where we went or what we did was not as important as the fact that we had time alone together so that we could talk and listen and have time for uninterrupted communication. With as large a family as we have and limited time to give to each individual child, you can see that "special time" comes only every 10 to 12 weeks for any one child. It is a time very important to our children.

Please know that we are not saying that this is the only significant time a parent can spend with his children; but rather we are saying to take advantage of every opportunity you have to spend special time together with each child.

When children grow up in a home where their mother and father demonstrate love to each other, where they receive unconditional love as expressed through eye and physical contact, and focused attention, they will want to have a relationship with their parents and hold dearly the Christian world view.

Teach Your Children!

The line separating good from evil and right from wrong has been blurred by the secular world view. We cannot count on the teachings of Sunday School to counteract the effect of the secular world view. We, as parents and educators, must consciously be teaching our children the implications of the Biblical world view in all aspects of life. Teaching our children to reason from the Biblical world view will give them the ability to judge the thoughts and ideas of the culture.

God through Moses has instructed parents how to teach their children:

> These are the commands, decrees and laws the Lord your God directed me to teach you to observe in the land that you are crossing the Jordan to possess, so that you, your children and their children after them may fear the Lord your God as long as you live by keeping all his decrees and commands that I give you and so that you may enjoy long life. Hear, O Israel, and be careful to obey so that it may go well with you and that you may increase greatly in a land flowing with milk and honey, just as the Lord, the God of your fathers promised you. Hear, O Israel: the Lord our God, the Lord is one. Love the Lord your God with all your heart and with all your soul and with all your strength. These commandments that I give you today are to be upon your hearts. Impress them on your children. Talk about them when you sit at home and when you walk along the road, when you lie down and when you get up" (Deuteronomy 6:1-7).

Teaching is not to be some cold theoretical theology. Moses explains that it is to be natural conversations between a father and son or daughter. If parents do not exercise their God-given assignment when their children are young, they cannot expect to have a mature relationship with them later. Edith Schaeffer explains that "Children are not to be told 'run along and don't ask questions.' Children are to be included in family discussion concerning the law of God and past history related in God's revelation. They are also to be included as the family studies God's Word as it relates to current things that are discussed during breakfast, as the morning paper is being read, or on a walk as the day's events are thought of ... God's law, God's Word, the Ten Commandments are to be related to the present moment of history, because these are the living Words of God and applicable right to the very end of the age ... And they should be a natural part of conversation."[7]

Each Child is Unique!

We must become students of our children. We must know our children intimately — their talents, their abilities, their hopes, and dreams. As we spend time with our children, we will know their hearts.

When it comes to writing this letter, we must emphasize that we cannot apply mechanical rules in this area of life anymore than we can in any other area. We, of all people, should realize this. As Christians we believe that our God is personal and infinite. According to modern thinking, men are only machines to be programmed, but to Christians personality really does exist and is important. We have been sharing general ideas; there are no automatic formulas. Because we are personal, each child is different. We must look to the Lord in prayer and to the work of the Holy Spirit for wisdom and understanding of each of our children. The letter that God is writing on the heart of each child is unique.

Some letters will be sent into the fine arts, offering hope where currently there is despair. Others will be sent into economics, encouraging the compassionate use of wealth. There will be other letters mailed to the sciences to redirect research and technical applications back to the dignity of man. Though all the letters will be as diverse as the beautiful array of flowers seen in a lovely garden, they all will speak of the life of Christ and the truth of Christianity!

Example to our Children!

It is often said that Christ is our example and that we should follow His example. In what way is Jesus our example? The answer to this question will give us direction as parents as to how we are to be an example to our children. How did Jesus live? In His own power, in His own strength, in His own wisdom? Not at all! Jesus made it very clear that apart from the Father He could do nothing (John 5:19, 30; 8:28). He lived in utter dependence upon the Father. He lived as man was originally created to live as the image bearer of God. When the people saw Jesus behaving, they didn't see the Second Person of the Trinity. Rather, they saw the Father. How do we know this? Listen to the conversation between Phillip and Jesus. "Phillip said to Him, "Lord, show us the Father, and it is enough for us. Jesus said to him, "Have I been so long with you, and yet you have not come to know Me, Phillip? He who has seen Me has seen the Father; how do you say, 'Show us the Father'? Do you not believe that I am in the Father, and the Father is in Me? The words that I say to you I do not speak on My own initiative, but the Father abiding in Me does His works. Believe Me that I am in the Father, and the Father in me; otherwise believe on account of the works themselves" (John 14: 8-11). Jesus, the Son of God, lived in complete and utter dependence upon the Father. Later in the conversation Jesus explains that "apart from Me you can do nothing" (John 15:5).

We are to live in dependence upon Christ just as Christ lived in dependence upon the Father. Just as those who saw the Father behaving when they saw the Son, our children will see Christ behaving when they look at us. Not because we are super Christians; not because we try harder; not because of our commitment; but rather, because Christ has clothed His deity in our humanity!

Before we can properly disciple our children, *our* lives must first be changed by the life and power of Christ. It is important that we follow the proper order. First, we must enter into *true spirituality* before we can lead our families to be *by faith families*. Then as we are *by faith families*, we will partner with God in the writing of this *letter of Christ*.

However, as parents *we feel* nine days out of ten incapable of doing all that is required of us. That is exactly where God wants us to be. It is then that we can agree with the Apostle Paul that our adequacy is not of ourselves, but rather our adequacy is from God (II Corinthians 3:5). It is then that we realize that we can no longer draw from our own limited resources, but rather we must draw from the unlimited resources of the risen Christ who empowers us to accomplish His will. We heartily agree with Paul ... "Not I but Christ!"

We must begin to think of our children as our major disciples. Our children are the ones God has given us the greatest opportunity to influence. *Do not miss this wonderful opportunity!* God has called us to entrust the revealed mystery of Christ in us to those within our sphere of influence — and our influence should reach into the third and fourth generation.

CAT'S IN THE CRADLE,[8] a song written during the 1960's, illustrates the negative consequences of our example as parents:

Cat's in the Cradle

A child just arrived the other day,
Came to the world in the usual way.
But there were planes to catch, bills to pay,
He learned to walk while I was away.
And he was talking before I knew it and as he grew he'd say
"I'm going to be like you Dad ... You know I'm going to be like you."

And the cat's in the cradle and the silver spoon,
Little boy blue and the man in the moon.
When you coming home Dad I don't know when
We'll get to together then — You know we'll have a good time then.

My son turned ten just the other day.
He said, "Thanks for the ball, Dad.
"Come on lets play. Can you teach me to throw?"
I said, "Not today! I got a lot to do."
He said, "That's OK."
And he walked away, but his smile never dimmed.
He said "I'm going be like him yea —
    You know I'm going to be like him."

And the cat's in the cradle and the silver spoon,
Little boy blue and the man in the moon.
When you coming home Dad I don't know when,
We'll get to together then — You know we'll have a good time then.

Well, he came from college just the other day
So much like a man that I just had to say,
"I am so proud of you. Can you sit for a while?"
He shook his head and said with a smile,
"What I would really like, Dad, is to borrow the car keys.
See you later. Can I have them, please?"

And the cat's in the cradle and the silver spoon,
Little boy blue and the man in the moon.
When you coming home, son, I don't know when.
We'll get to together then, Dad -
You know we'll have a good time then.

I have long since retired and my son has moved away.
Called him up just the other day.
I said, "I'd like to see you if you don't mind."
He said, "I'd like to, Dad, if I can find the time.
You see, my new job is a hassle and my kids have the flu.
But it is sure nice talking to you, Dad,
It is sure nice talking to you."

As I hung up the phone it occurred to me
He'd grown up just like me!
My boy was just like me!

And the cat's in the cradle and the silver spoon,
Little boy blue and the man in the moon.
When you coming home son I don't know when.
We'll get to together then, Dad,
We are going to have a good time then.

IN AS MUCH AS *God has called us to discipleship; and,*
FURTHERMORE, *since there is no greater calling than leading
your own children to Christ and building them in the faith so that
they will impact the next generation for Christ;*

THEREFORE, LET US HIGHLY RESOLVE
*to carefully and conscientiously prepare and care for this "Letter of
Christ" written by the Spirit of the living God which will be read
by those of the 21st century.*

Resolve Number Seven

To Challenge The Culture With The Truth Of Christianity And The Life Of Christ

"We are destroying speculations and every lofty thing raised up against the knowledge of God, and we are taking every thought captive to the obedience of Christ."

— 2 Corinthians 10:5

Our responsibility as Christians is to challenge what is not real and true in our society with what is true. An emphasis on thinking (truth) and living (character) is tremendously needed at present.[1]

— What in the World is Real?

Are you teaching your children that Christianity is a system of thought that applies to all of life? Are they being educated to be a generation that will vigorously resist humanistic values and infringement on their rights? Are you guiding your children to help them understand twentieth-century problems so the coming generation will know how to attack the desperate crisis we face from a Christian [world view]?[2]

— John Whitehead

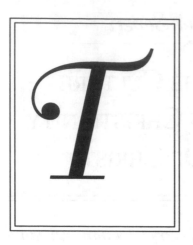

he battle lines are drawn. The Judeo-Christian world view is in the cross fire of the culture. What are we to do? Should we only be interested in the "soul" of the individual and let the culture go its own way? Do we pull back from society and isolate ourselves from the culture, or do we prepare our families to destroy "speculations ... raised up against the knowledge of God"

(II Corinthians 10:4-5)? Just how are we as Christians to relate to the culture in which we live?

Imagine purchasing a beautiful new floor lamp. It is delivered the next day in a packing box. You set it in your living room. Everyone sits around the box admiring it. The room light begins to dim as evening approaches. Everyone is thinking, "What a beautiful box." Someone asks, "Has the lamp been plugged in?" Realizing it has not, you cut an opening in the bottom of the box in order to pull out the cord. You plug it into the outlet.

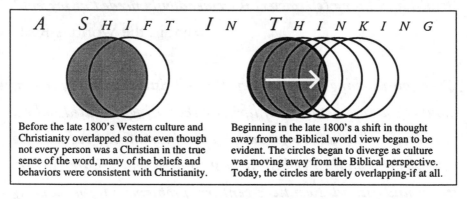

A   S H I F T   I N   T H I N K I N G

Before the late 1800's Western culture and Christianity overlapped so that even though not every person was a Christian in the true sense of the word, many of the beliefs and behaviors were consistent with Christianity.

Beginning in the late 1800's a shift in thought away from the Biblical world view began to be evident. The circles began to diverge as culture was moving away from the Biblical perspective. Today, the circles are barely overlapping-if at all.

Everyone continues to admire the box as the room grows darker and darker. Jesus said that a city set upon a hill could not be hidden and that we are the light of the world (Matthew 5:14,15). Isolating ourselves does not seem to be what He has called us to do. In fact, we are called ambassadors for Christ (2 Corinthians 5:20). What does an ambassador do? He represents the thoughts and ideas — the policy — of the country in which he represents. While it might be nice to be an ambassador to England or France, what about being an ambassador to a hostile country like Iran or Libya? We must equip our children to stand independent of the thoughts and ideas of the secular world view so that they will not be influenced by its thinking. We must prepare our children to represent the life of Christ and the truth of Christianity to the culture in which God is sending them. They are the letter of Christ to be read by all men!

There was a time in which the cultural view of the world overlapped the Judeo-Christian world view. While this congruency may have made it a little easier to live with less tension and less conflict, people could "pretend" to be Christian. Today because the issues are becoming black and white, the contrast allows the light of Christianity to shine more brightly. Monumental shifts in thinking occurred during the last three decades of the 1800's. While the epicenter of these shifts can be traced to changes in the philosophical ideas of the last century, the associated tremors during this century changed to major quakes in our general culture during the 1960's. Western culture was turned upside down.

The Predominant Map

Because different world views provide different answers to life's most basic questions, they can not coexist in the same society for long. The transition from one view to another usually results in tremendous conflict. On a trip to Indiana we stopped to observe the Ohio and Wabash Rivers. We noticed each of them flowing smoothly. There was a sense of peace and tranquility. As we went a little further, we saw something quite different. The waters were very turbulent. What was the difference? We were at the place where the two rivers were merging! Two mighty forces were clashing against each other. Which river would dominate the other?

A culture cannot gain or maintain equilibrium by holding to two different views of life. It normally seeks an equilibrium by embracing one view or another. During certain times in history one world view is dominant over the other. Just as the Ohio River overpowered the Wabash River, one world view eventually becomes the predominant map of culture.

Two of the easiest ways to see which world view is predominant at a specific time in history is to look at the art or listen to the music of the culture. For example, trace art through history beginning from second or third century Christian art to modern twentieth century art. What you see is a series of shifts away from as well as toward a Biblical world view. Rembrandt, for example, painting out of the Biblical base, was able to paint the poor as well as the rich, children as well as adults, the beautiful and not so beautiful. He was able to balance form (technique) with content. He did not need to drift into any dreamlike unreality. Why? His map of life or his world view said that all people are important because all people are created in the image of God. Picasso, on the other hand, rejected the Biblical base for his life and showed life as distorted, fragmented, and broken apart.

The shift away from the Biblical world view began in the late 1800's. It has taken quite a while actually to change the consensus of our Judeo-Christian culture. However, during the last 30 years the Biblical world view has been systematically replaced.

Picture your kitchen table. With all four legs on the floor the table is stable; the place settings and bouquet are all secure. That was our culture with the Biblical base as the foundation for our culture. The shift away from this world view is like tilting the table. At first the shift did not affect the general culture and it was thus not really perceived. The shift had occurred even though it was not noticed by the general population. However, during the 1960's and 1970's this change began to affect the general culture; the table was being tilted to an extreme, and the place settings and bouquet began to move. Everything was being rearranged. General culture was being set upon the secular surface. The four legs holding up this table are *modernism* (the belief that there is no God), *naturalism* (the belief that there is no supernatural dimension to life), *evolution* (the belief that time, chance, and natural processes have "created" the world) and *determinism* (the belief that man can be programmed like a machine or conditioned like an animal).

In the last thirty years the Biblical world view and the Secular world view have been in conflict. The two world views are competing for the control of our culture, and therefore the minds of our children. As the twentieth century comes to a close, two powerful sets of ideas are clashing, like two mighty rivers!

This clashing culture is the one in which our children are being raised. There is a spiritual battle that is happening in the physical realm. We must, therefore, adequately prepare our children to stand independent of the secular world view and dependent upon Jesus Christ and the Truth of Christianity. John Whitehead [3] challenges Christians to be teaching our children that *Christianity is a system of thought that applies to all of life.* We must not isolate Christianity to any one part of life. All of life must be under the Lordship of Jesus Christ. There must not be any artificial separation of Christianity and the rest of life. Second, he insists that our children must be educated *to be a generation that will vigorously resist humanistic values and infringement on their rights.* They must resolve to be like Daniel and not defile themselves by accepting the beliefs offered by the secular society. They must be able to stand against the thoughts and ideas of the secular culture. And finally, Whitehead exhorts us to be *guiding our children to help them understand twentieth century problems so the coming generation will know how to attack the desperate crisis we face from a Christian world view.*

Confronting the Culture with the Truth of Christianity

Paul says that we are "to be destroying speculations and every lofty thing raised up against the knowledge of God, and ... taking every thought captive to the obedience of Christ (II Corinthians 10:5)." It is imperative that we underscore that Paul did not say to destroy people who hold different beliefs! We must become skilled at destroying the false ideas that people are basing their lives upon without destroying the people. If we do not destroy these false ideas, these false ideas will destroy the people! "A fundamental part of our calling," explains Jerram Barrs, "is to demolish arguments and every pretention that sets itself up against the true knowledge of God, and to take captive every thought to make it obedient to Christ."[4]

Imagine driving late at night onto a bridge that has collapsed. Your car overturns, but no one is seriously injured. You gain your senses and start walking back down the highway. You see other cars coming. Will you let them find out for themselves that the bridge is out, or will you do everything in your power to stop them? Of course, out of compassion for other members of the human race (even though, you have never met these people), you will try to keep them from the impending disaster. The young people of our culture have been told that there is no God, that there are no absolutes, that everything is relative, that whatever you want to do is okay, that there are no consequences to their decisions! This is the collapsed bridge and many are now dying. What can or should we do?

People holding to these beliefs must be confronted with the truth of Christianity in order to come into a personal relationship with Christ. You see, their map, their table top, their world view is not reality. Remember the little line:

Row, row, row your boat gently down the stream.

Merrily, merrily, merrily, merrily life is but a dream.

Reality is not "but a dream!" This secular table top is not reality! What then can we do or say to the many thousands of people who are resting their lives upon this unstable, secular surface?

Does it really matter which set of ideas, which world view a person or culture holds to be true? Can it really make that much difference? Jesus said that you shall know them by their fruit. A good tree bears good fruit and cannot bear bad fruit. Likewise a bad tree can not produce good fruit, but rather bears bad fruit. What is the fruit of each world view? What affect has the Biblical world view had upon society? What about the secular view? What are the implications of life that arise from either the Biblical world view or the secular view? Is there a basis for judging the direction in which the culture has moved? Is there an absolute standard that can be used to measure the ideas that are being proposed?

Art and Music

In the arena of art, look at the works of Van Eyck, Durer, or Rembrandt. (To understand what we are talking about you must really go to a museum or at least check out art books from the library.) These men were working from the Biblical base, and you can see their fruits.

Now what about the secular view? What are its fruits? In art we have Picasso, Pollock, and others working out of *the new way of thinking*. What have they contributed to the beauty of life through art? Pollock working out of the belief that man, the highest form of animal life, was the result of time, chance, and impersonal natural processes (evolution) conceived that these same three processes would produce the highest form of art. And so in *Lavender Mist*[5] he placed the canvas horizontally on the floor, placed buckets of paint on ropes and pulleys above the canvas. He then pushed the buckets across the canvas and out splashed the paint. The work hangs in the National Gallery of Art in Washington, D.C. The National Gallery's

Director Emeritus, John Walker, explains that in "parts of Pollock's best works...one finds [a beauty similar to] a piece of drapery by Botticelli or tresses of hair by Leonardo."[6] Does that sound absurd? Remember, this is the new way of thinking! These are the fruits of modern beliefs.

Does time, chance, and impersonal natural processes produce "higher forms" of art than those built upon the base of the reality of God? The fruits of modern despair and hopelessness are for all to see and hear while those built upon the Biblical world view show richness and beauty, orderliness and structure. Let us, therefore, highly resolve to teach our children to appreciate and create that which reflects the character and nature of God — not the despair of man separated from Him.

Concerning classical music, listen to works by Johann Sebastian Bach, Georg Friedrich Handel, Felix Mendelssohn or Johannes Brahms. Bach often wrote upon his score of music "To God Be the Glory." His music was the outworking of a set of ideas based upon his belief, the Biblical world view. He did not separate his music into sacred and secular. Many of his works were dedicated to glorify God. To these composers order, structure, and patterns reflected the nature and character of God. When conflict was introduced, these composers brought final resolution. Contrast the beautiful melodies of Bach, Handel, or Haydn with influential twentieth-century composers Gustav Mahler, Arnold Schoenberg, or John Cage.

According to Leonard Bernstein in the *Norton Lectures* at Harvard University in 1973 "ours is a century of death and Mahler is its musical prophet...If Mahler knew this [personal death, death of tonality, then death of culture as it had been] and his message is so clear, how do we knowing it too, manage to survive?"[7]

John Cage said that one of his greatest works of music came as a result of selecting 15 pebbles from his oriental garden. He set each pebble onto the score. He proceeded to trace around each pebble. The musicians were then to play round each pebble. Another time he placed a very large aquarium on the stage. The empty score was drawn across the face of the aquarium glass. He had angel fish in the tank. The musicians were to follow the angel fish and play the notes as the fish moved up and down the score! While the music of Bach, and Handel brings great beauty and joy, the latter brings the macabre and despair.

I once saw a musical activity written for gifted and talented students in a public school. The title, *You Too Can Compose Like Mozart* caught my eye. I was quickly shocked to read that the child was to roll two dice and add the values together. If the number two was rolled, then the child would mark middle C on the score. If the number three was rolled, then C# would be marked on the score. This same by chance process was to be continued until the piece was finished. What a deception. The more Shirley and I thought about this activity the more outraged we became. This was not the way composers working from the Judeo-Christian consensus of order, structure, and pattern thought. This dice activity reflects the chance philosophy of evolution and modernism! This technique does not produce beautiful music, but rather clanging noises!

The *Concise Oxford Dictionary of Music* explains "from the point of view of any 19th century musician, Harmony [in the 20th century] is now in a state of anarchy...."[8] There was a shift in thought that occurred during the final decades of the last century. This shift from the Biblical world view to the secular view point has seeped into all of life. Discord is now thought to be harmony! Atonality is believed to be tonality. According to Edward Gibbon in *Decline and Fall of the Roman Empire* one of the characteristics of Rome at its end was a "freakishness in the arts, masquerading as originality and enthusiasms pretending to be creativity."[9] In an attempt to justify 20th century classical music the *Oxford Dictionary* continues: "but a kinder way (and perhaps wiser) to speak of [20th century music] as passing through a stage of bold experimentation."[10]

Donald Grout, in his book *A History of Western Music*, explains the development of four basic characteristics of classical music that began to take shape in the eleventh century. These four characteristics include: composition, notation, principles of order, and polyphony. Listen to his description of twentieth century classical music:

> ...we can see that some developments in the twentieth century have altered three of them almost out of recognition. *Composition*, in the sense of existence of a work of music apart from any particular performance, has in some quarters given way to controlled improvisation (which was the practice in antiquity and the early Middle Ages). As to *notation*, the score in many cases is now no longer a definitive set of directions; the performer instead being only a

mediator between composer and audience, has become himself to a great extent the composer (again, as in the early Middle Ages). *Principles of order* have changed — arguably, the change is greater than any within the whole previous eight hundred years; and, if we think of total indeterminacy, principles of order have simply ceased to exist. Only *polyphony* remains. In view of all this, it seems not too much to say that the twentieth century has witnessed a musical revolution in the full sense of the word.[11]

Grout further explains that modern man is "isolated, helpless in the grip of forces he does not understand, prey to inner conflict, tension, anxiety, fear, and all the elemental irrational drives of the subconscious, and in irritated rebellion against established order and accepted forms."[12] Twentieth century classical music based upon the secular world view is describing the modern world and modern man without God.

Although Beethoven [13] believed in a Fate philosophy of life, much of his music was constrained by the Christian consensus of his time. Because the Biblical world view was the base on which people set their lives, those not holding to that view were in many cases functioning as if they did. In Romans 12: 1-2, Paul exhorts:

> I urge you therefore, brethren, by the mercies of God, to present your bodies a living sacrifice, acceptable to God, which is your spiritual service of worship. And do not be conformed to this world, but be transformed by the renewing of your mind that you may prove what the will of God is, that which is good and acceptable and perfect.

As Christians living in a secular culture, let us highly resolve to be transformed by the renewing of our minds so that what we create will reflect the true nature and character of God. Christians must beware not to create music or art that is constrained by the secular view rather than reflect the true nature and character of God. Let us also highly resolve to teach our children to enjoy, discern, and appreciate that which is truly lovely and beautiful so that they will turn away from that which is shallow and twisted.

Our Language

A curious thing has happened in our country regarding our language. The affect of the secular fragmentation has chipped away even here. "I hope you enjoy your meal this evening" once spoken by a waiter or waitress has now become "Enjoy!" The Dr. Seuss generation stands in sharp contrast to the past. Modern experts tell us that children have too short of an attention span to understand let alone enjoy books having long complicated sentence structures. However, in the 1948 children's classic *Blueberries for Sal*[14] by Robert McCloskey we read "Her mother went back to her picking, but Little Sal, because her feet were tired of standing and walking, sat down in the middle of a large clump of bushes and ate blueberries." Did you count the words in this sentence! There are 33 words!

And then there is the word "cool." How is it used today? What does it mean? *Relating to the temperature; wonderful; unique; good; bad!* The list could go on and on. Creative spelling is the next movement toward the destruction of our language. Remember e e cummings! He is one of the significant people illustrating the *new way of thinking* proposed by Hillary Clinton. Secular thinking does not build up; rather, it destroys. It is twisting that which was beautiful. Gene-Stratton Porter makes this comment regarding our language:

> The last thing that I want to mention in these high resolves is that you and I and everyone in this country shall make an attempt to use the English language correctly, shall make an effort in our daily work and conversation, in the books and papers we read aloud everywhere we go, to give to the people the dignity, the superior cultural effect that can be attained by any man or woman who arises and opens his or her mouth and speaks nicely accented, clearly pronounced, deliberately constructed sentences in the English language. If we allow a flood of slang to overwhelm us, if we allow the spelling of our language to be jazzed as our music is being, if we forget ourselves and chatter like a flock of swallows over a smoking chimney, we shall continue to be the spectacle in the future that we have been in the past when we attempt to express our thoughts and there emanates from our mouths a jargon deleted of endings, wrongly accented, some-

times three and four words run into one, very frequently saying precisely the opposite of what we mean or intend to say. Naturally, it is only possible for each one of us to do the best we can, but for the love of pride, for the sake of abolishing the spectacle we make before other nations, let each and every one of us highly resolve to speak the level best brand of English that we are capable of uttering.[15]

Science, Medicine, and Technology

Do science and Scripture conflict? Newton, Boyle, Maxwell... and many other founders of modern science would have said "No!" Modern science actually had its birth in Christianity.

Today while some doctors spend enormous amounts of energy in the emergency room to save a child, an unborn child is aborted in the room next door. How can these two positions stand side-by-side? Modern science, though born out of a Christian world view, has given rise to a technology utilized by the secular world view. Medicine under the influence of the Christian world view valued and chose life not death. The dignity of man, as we have known it, is unique to Western civilization. This dignity rests exclusively upon the view that man is made in the "image of God." When God was removed from our society, so was man's dignity. That is why more that 4,000 innocent babies are killed each day through abortion in the United States of America. We must highly resolve to restore the proper view of man into the culture. When man is no longer reduced to the level of an animal or machine, then such atrocities will stop.

Government

What about governments? Is one form of government superior to another? Is government considered the fundamental entity of society or are the people? A redefining of government is currently taking place.

For example, would you consider the three branches of our government a system of checks-and-balances or an archaic system resulting in continuous grid-lock? Would it not be a lot easier to accomplish the task of governing if these three branches were under one person or a small ruling elite? Why did the Founding Fathers of the United States of America so painstakingly persist in separating these three powers?

It was their view of man that guided and directed their thinking. What was their view of man and what source did they draw upon in shaping their understanding? They believed in the total depravity of man. Although they believed God created man in an ideal state, man rebelled from his Creator. He is by nature sinful. Of course, this view of man is the Biblical world view. It is interesting to note that "The source most often cited by the Founding Fathers, was the Bible, which accounted for 34 percent of all citations."[16] One's view of human nature does significantly influence one's view of government. Knowing from Divine Revelation that the basic tendency of man is toward power and control because of the fall of man, our own Founding Fathers wisely separated the powers typical of a king into the legislative, executive, and judicial branches. "First, they recognized that the government must be powerful enough to restrain the evil impulses of the masses….But they also recognized that rulers possess sinful natures. Therefore rulers cannot be trusted with absolute power….So most of the problems the founders of the U.S. Constitution were faced with when they gathered at the Great Convention in 1787 had to do with setting up checks and balances relating to sin and power."[17] However, when the view of man changes, the system of "checks and balances" is considered "grid-lock". When a person hopes to set himself above the law in order to erect his own *American Agenda*, the Constitutional boundaries become confining. It is hard to believe that the 104th Congress had to pass a law stating that they would place themselves under the law of the land!

What can be said of other governments? Such men as Lenin, Stalin, and Hitler sought to enslave and control people through crisis, fear and pain. All these men, working out of a secular set of ideas, left the emptiness, pain, silence, and violence of their world view for all to see. Let us, therefore, highly resolve to reclaim our American heritage so that history will not be rewritten, and our children and our grandchildren will not be enslaved to the secular system of thought.

Giving Direction to the Culture with the Truth of Christianity

Does it really then make any difference what set of ideas, what beliefs, what presuppositions a person, or culture accepts as true? Yes, the world view held to be true drastically affects the outcomes of all disciplines of life. History clearly allows us to see that "you shall know them by their fruits."

Looking at life from the Biblical world view allows us to analyze and evaluate the culture. The Biblical world view provides an absolute moral standard based upon the nature and character of God; therefore, we have a fixed reference point, a gauge against which we can judge the thoughts, ideas, and decisions of the culture. This gauge leads us to give insight into the many problems we face together as a human race.

Like a magnificent tapestry interwoven with gold, scarlet, and lavender strands of thread, Western civilization creates a wonderful picture. All woven fabrics consist of horizontal and vertical threads. In an ordinary woven fabric the horizontal and vertical threads can both be seen. However, in a tapestry, the horizontal threads completely conceal the vertical ones. History is like a tapestry. The horizontal threads of history are the interweaving of art, music, philosophy, theology, science, government, and economics. The vertical threads are the world view held by the culture. Depending upon which world view is held to be true at a particular point in history, the tapestry either holds together or it begins to unravel.

To give adequate and appropriate solutions to 21st century problems, we must know the correct cause. If we attribute the problem to an incorrect cause, then the proposed solution will be either inadequate or inappropriate. Take, for example, the problem of drugs. What is the cause of this problem? Some say that it is a lack of knowledge. The line of reasoning goes something like this: If people just know the negative affects of drugs, then they will stop. If this reasoning is true, then it follows that drug education is the appropriate solution. Plato believed that morally "bad" choices are made because of a lack of knowledge. What does the Biblical world view say about making morally "bad" choices? Lack of knowledge certainly contributes. The law was given to show us our sin. However, the cause goes deeper than a lack of knowledge. Bad choices stem from our separation from God. Therefore, only to educate a person is like putting a bandage on a person who needs a tourniquet. Solutions based upon the Biblical world view will be appropriate to what is the real cause of man's problems.

In addition to giving insight into problems of our culture, our children, as "letters of Christ" to the culture, must be faithful to their own world view. As we approach the 21st century, it is no time to retreat from culture. Our children must be taught to resist compromising Christian thought with secular ideas.

We have a rich Western heritage based upon the Biblical world view. The zenith of Western civilization in music, art, science, government, and literature occurred with the Biblical world view as its base. Bach, Rembrandt, Newton, Rutherford, and Milton were all working in each of their respective disciplines out of the Biblical world view. Because modernism has not produced what modernists hoped, our children must take the lead in returning each of the disciplines to the Lordship of Christ. Our children need to know how to express the Christian world view in compelling ways to modern culture. *As their ideas are applied in the various fields of study, they will be the light shining in our current darkness. This is a vital part of the 21st century apologetic.*

Confronting the Culture with the Person of Christ

If our objective is simply to restructure our culture, we have missed the mark. If future historians write that we changed the structure of culture but the people of the culture did not come to know Christ, then we will have failed miserably. Neither is our purpose in talking with someone about Christ and Christianity to win an argument. You may ask why then take the time to understand the world views and their implications into life? Understanding life from a world view perspective should enable our children to build bridges of conversation between themselves and the people of the 21st century culture.

Some people are simply ready to receive Christ. They believe that there is a personal-infinite God; they recognize they have a real need; they are ready to believe, but they need to know how to enter into this relationship. Don't burden them with long conversations. Simply lead them to our loving heavenly Father who eagerly awaits them.

Some other people believe in God and moral absolutes, but have legitimate questions that need to be answered. They may have some questions about the authority of the Bible, or maybe they need to understand the uniqueness of Jesus. We must not only know what we believe but also why we believe what we believe. We must always be ready "in season and out of season" (II Timothy 4:2) to give "an adequate defense for the hope that we have within us, with gentleness and reverence" (I Peter 3:15). As we are helping them with the answers to their questions, our foremost aim is to assist them in seeing how to enter into a personal relationship with God.

Unfortunately there will be many other people who will see no need for God. The secularization of our culture is raising a new generation of nonbelieving Americans. According to a special edition of *Time* [18] magazine: *Beyond the Year 2000,* school children of the 21st century are predicted not to have any knowledge nor interest in spiritual matters. Personal references to God will be shunned. This is an example of the *new way of thinking.* This new godless culture is the one in which our children are being raised and in which God is calling them to be light. There are a growing number of people in our post-Christian culture who have accepted the idea that there is no God. Many such people are today shaping and making public policies which continue to remove God further and further from our culture. To tell a person who has accepted this *new way of thinking* as truth that what he has been taught is not reality but only a shadow will make little or no sense to him. The following is a paraphrase of the cave analogy by Plato:

> A cave is described in which a number of men are held captive. The men are tied up in such a way that they can only look straight ahead. All they can see then are shadows projected onto the wall of the cave. Since the prisoners never see anything but these shadows they think that the shadows on the wall are real. Nothing else exists for them. Suddenly then one of the prisoners is freed and makes his way out of the cave immerging into the sunlight. The change is difficult for the freed man. At first he refuses to look at the new world around him. *If he were compelled to look at the light itself, would not that pain his eyes. And would he not turn away and flee to those things he is able to discern in the shadows and regard them as more clear and more exact than the objects illuminated by the sun.* Gradually however the freed prisoner recognizes that the images he'd seen on the cave wall were indeed only shadows of the world that he now sees so clearly. Reluctantly, he returns to the cave to tell the other prisoners about his discovery, but they refuse to believe him. They know only the world of shadows. They have no reason to doubt this world is real. In fact, they resent

the returning prisoner and the news he brings of another reality. He wants them to give up their traditional beliefs. There is a difference between the world of shadows and the real world.[19]

Those prisoners, having lived their whole existence in the shadows of the cave, are convinced that their experiential knowledge is truly real. Jesus said that "while seeing they do not see, and while hearing they do not hear, nor do they understand" (Matthew 13:13).

What are we to do or say to these prisoners of the secular viewpoint? Can we converse with them about Christ or does the conversation just end? We must be preparing our children to converse with this growing segment of our culture. But how? What can we say?

Remember the maps? The Biblical world view accurately guides us to our destination. *Who am I? Where am I from?* and *Where am I going?* Biblical truth gives us the proper directions to these and other questions. Even though the secular map may lead a person to some immediate pleasure, it will eventually lead them to destruction. When our children meet and begin conversing with a person who has based his life upon this secular map, what are they to say? You might think they could simply say, "You have the wrong map" and then offer them the true map. However, we do not think it will be quite that easy.

Remember, they are really in darkness and have been deceived into believing this to be the true map. Return once again to Prince Rilian in the *Silver Chair* [20] by C. S. Lewis. The Witch, having thrown some magical green powder into the fire, begins to talk and strum her instrument monotonously. "Narnia...There is no land called Narnia." As the conversation continues, the children become enchanted. They are convinced that Narnia is but a dream — that it does not exist. Then one remembers the sun. They all agree that yes, there is a sun. Then the Queen of the underworld challenges this belief. She asks what they mean by the sun. What is it like? They say that it is like a lamp hung in the sky. She counters with her view that their sun is but a dream. "There is nothing in that dream that was not copied from the lamp. The lamp is the real thing.; the sun is but a tale, a children's story." The truth is replaced with a lie. The children are brought back under the evil spell.

The non-Christian children of the 21 st century are being "enchanted" to believe the secular map is true. They have been taught this map from their earliest days and have believed and followed it for years. It has numbed their thinking of reality. At first it gives some sense of security and some pleasure. We must help them use their minds to follow their map to its final destination. If they are in the fine arts, we must help them see what the art they embrace says about man. If they are in science, we must help them see what their map says about the structure of the universe or the uniqueness of man. The secular map is a false map of reality. It is a distorted image of what is real. Taking a person to the logical conclusion of his thinking will bring him to a point of feeling uncomfortable in his thinking. This approach will enable us to talk with him about the inadequacy of his map and the possibility of other maps.

Our approach must be done carefully. We must help them see that following the secular map will bring destruction to their personal lives as well as to the culture. The secular map eventually leads to the collapsed bridge. We do not want them to crash. We must warn them. When a person sees the end, he will be ready to accept the idea that his map is incorrect. Then he may be open to considering other maps. Then our children must be ready to explain to them the Biblical world view. Our map gives good, sufficient, and adequate answers to life's basic questions. It will lead to fulfillment, purpose, and meaning in life as the person enters into the proper Creator-creature relationship. We *do* have something to say, something of great importance to the children of the 21st century. We must be adequately preparing and equipping our children to converse with those of the 21st century.

IN AS MUCH AS *Christianity is a system of thought that applies to all aspects of life; and*

FURTHERMORE, *since Christianity gives the only absolute standard by which to measure the thoughts and ideas of a culture;*

THEREFORE LET US HIGHLY RESOLVE

to challenge the culture with the truth of Christianity and the life of Jesus Christ.

WE DO NOT LOSE HEART

"Therefore, since we have this ministry, as we received mercy, we do not lose heart ... But we have this treasure in earthen vessels, that the surpassing greatness of the power may be of God and not from ourselves."

— 2 Corinthians 4: 1,7

What is lacking at the present minute in music, in art, in literature, in our schools, in our churches, in our moving pictures, in our civic government is merely the courage of our [Biblical] convictions.[1]

— Gene Stratton-Porter

lthough the call and challenge to prepare our children to enter into the 21st century is your desire, does it seem beyond what you can do? Do you have the feeling that 20th century life has completely eliminated any time for family life? Do you feel totally exhausted at the end of the day? At this pace, do you wonder how you can possibly keep going? Do you ever feel like giving up and throwing in the towel?

Choosing to disciple our families is not easy physically, emotionally, or spiritually. There never seems to be enough time in the day to finish all that is necessary. It is tempting to delegate it to someone else. Is it any wonder that such pressures can cause us to "lose heart"? What is it that anchors us to this ministry?

NOT LOSING HEART

"Therefore, since we have this ministry, as we received mercy, we do not **lose heart** ... But we have this treasure in earthen vessels, that the surpassing greatness of the power may be of God and not from ourselves" (2 Corinthians 4:1, 7). The process of discipling our children is truly a ministry. What does Paul say about not losing heart? It was God's mercy that kept him from losing heart so that he could point to God as the source for the power not to give up. He describes this power as "surpassing greatness." The word used for power in this passage is the same word that is used for our word *dynamite*! Note, too, the source for this power. It is from God — not ourselves. When you feel like you have no strength for carrying on and you just want to give up, remember that your strength in Christ has the energy and power of dynamite, that is extra strength! Ask God to strengthen you in your inner man in Christ just as Paul prays for believers.

FOR ETERNITY

"We are afflicted in every way," says Paul, "but not crushed; perplexed, but not despairing; persecuted, but not forsaken; struck down, but not destroyed....Therefore we do not **lose heart**....For momentary, light affliction is producing for us an eternal weight of glory far beyond all comparison" (2 Corinthians 4:8,16-18). Take another look at the words he used to describe his circumstances — afflicted, perplexed, persecuted, struck down. Can you believe he calls that momentary, light affliction? Paul was looking to eternity with eyes of faith in the daily grind of life, knowing that the eternal glory far outweighed the physical, emotional, and financial hardships.

As we approach the 21st century, we must not faint. Rather, we must resolve to impart the courage of our Biblical convictions to our children. Jesus said that we are to "make disciples of all the nations...." *Begin with those over whom He has given you the greatest influence — your children!*

THEREFORE, LET US HIGHLY RESOLVE

- *To Build our Families upon the Biblical World View.*

- *To Establish our Children's Lives upon Truth and Absolutes.*

- *To Equip our Children to Reason.*

- *To Enter into True Spirituality.*

- *To Be "By Faith" Families.*

- *To Prepare our Children as a "Letter of Christ" to the Culture.*

- *To Challenge our Culture with the Truth of Christianity and the Life of Christ.*

We close with what we began — with the vision, the perspective, the high calling of preparing our families to enter the 21st century:

When I think of the life that we are leading, of the uses to which we have put the bounty provided for us by the Almighty, when I think of the greed and the lust and the selfishness that is crowding everything that is high and holy and delicate, that is kind and loving and considerate of our fellow men, from our hearts, I wish that I might attain to some high peak from which my voice could reach to the ends of the earth, and that there I might cry out to the men and women of my day and generation, to the men and women of whom we are the mothers and the fathers, and to the children that our children are rearing, I wish that I might cry out:

LET US HIGHLY RESOLVE

that we will do everything that our day and location permits actually to put into practice the teachings of Jesus Christ.[2]

— Notes —

PREFACE

1. Samuel Adams, speech given in 1771, as quoted in *Bartlett's Familiar Quotations: 16th Edition* (Boston: Little Brown and Company, 1992), p. 369.
2. Francis Schaeffer, *How Should We Then Live?* from *The Complete Works of Francis Schaeffer: A Christian Worldview* (Wheaton, Illinois: Crossway Books, 1982), Vol. 5, p. 84.
3. "Beyond the Year 2000: What to Expect in the New Millennium." *Time*, 1992.
4. Gene Stratton-Porter, *Let Us Highly Resolve* (London: Hutchinson and Co., Ltd.), pp. 278-279.

RESOLVE NUMBER ONE

1. Francis Schaeffer, *How Should We Then Live?* from *The Complete Works of Francis Schaeffer: A Christian Worldview* (Wheaton, Illinois: Crossway Books, 1982), Vol. 5, pp. 83-84.
2. Gladys Hunt, *Honey For A Child's Heart* (Grand Rapids, Michigan: Zondervan Publishing House, 1978), p. 95.
3. *Parade*, April 11, 1993, front page.
4. Ibid.
5. Francis Schaeffer, *How Should We Then Live?* from *The Complete Works of Francis Schaeffer: A Christian Worldview* (Wheaton, Illinois: Crossway Books, 1982), Vol. 5, p. 84.
6. James Sire, *How To Read Slowly: A Christian Guide to Reading with the Mind* (Downers Grove, Illinois: Inter Varsity Press, 1979), p. 14.
7. Johanna Spyri, *Heidi* (New York: Children's Classics, 1986), pp. 202-203.
8. Norman Grubb, *Rees Howells Intercessor* (Fort Washington, Pennsylvania: Christian Literature Crusade, 1987), p. 59.
9. Bill Clinton, *Dallas Morning News*, October 27, Section J, pp. 1, 10, 1996.
10. *Parade*, April 11, 1993.
11. "People Who Inspire Me." *Parade*, April 1993, p. 12.
12. *World Book Encyclopedia* (Chicago, Illinois: World Book, Inc. Vol. 3, 1985), p. 85
13. As quoted by William Federer, *America's God and Country: Encyclopedia of Quotations* (Coppell, Texas: FAME Publishing, Inc., 1994), p. 205.
14. *World Book Encyclopedia* (Chicago, Illinois: Field Enterprise Inc. Vol. 7 , 1953), p. 3099.
15. Francis Schaeffer, *The God Who Is There* from *The Complete Works of Francis Schaeffer: A Christian Worldview* (Wheaton, Illinois: Crossway Books, 1982), Vol. 1, p. 30.

RESOLVE NUMBER TWO

1. Robert Frost, *"The Road Not Taken"* from *You Come Too: Favorite Poems for Young Readers* (New York: Henry Holt and Company, 1959), p. 84.
2. Jerram Barrs, *What In The World Is Real: Challenging the Superficial in Today's World* (Champaign, Illinois: Communication Institute, 1982), pp. 30-31.
3. Edith Schaeffer, *Lifelines* (Wheaton, Illinois: Crossway Books, 1982), p. 18.

RESOLVE NUMBER THREE

1. Francis Schaeffer, *Back to Freedom and Dignity* from *The Complete Works of Francis Schaeffer: A Christian Worldview* (Wheaton, Illinois: Crossway Books, 1982), Vol. 1, p. 380.
2. George Lucas, *Star Wars*, Twentieth Century-Fox, Lucasfilm Ltd., 1977.
3. George Lucas, *The Empire Strikes Back*, Twentieth Century-Fox, Lucasfilm Ltd.,1980.
4. Francis Schaeffer, *Back to Freedom and Dignity* from *The Complete Works of Francis Schaeffer: A Christian Worldview* (Wheaton, Illinois: Crossway Books, 1982), Vol. 1, p. 376.
5. Ibid., p. 380
6. Francis Schaeffer, *Genesis in Space and Time* from *The Complete Works of Francis Schaeffer: A Christian Worldview* (Wheaton, Illinois: Crossway Books, 1982), Vol. 2, p. 49.
7. George Lucas, *Star Wars*, Twentieth Century-Fox, Lucasfilm Ltd.,1977.
8. Ibid.

9. George Lucas, *The Empire Strikes Back*, Twentieth Century-Fox, Lucasfilm Ltd., 1980.

10. B.F. Skinner, *Beyond Freedom and Dignity* (New York: Bantam Books, 1971), p. 191.

11. Michael Bond, *Paddington On Top* (Boston: Houghton Mifflin Company, 1974), p12.

12. Edmund Marek and David Quine, "Reasoning Abilities of Home-Educated Children," *Journal of Law, Ethics and Public Policy*, Vol. 3 Issue No. 4, 1988. pp 562 - 568.

13. Jean Piaget, "Intellectual Evolution from Adolescence to Adulthood." *Human Development* 15(1): 1-12, 1972.

14. John Renner and Edmund Marek, *The Learning Cycle* (Portsmouth, New Hampshire: Heinemann, 1988), p. 25.

15. Jean Piaget, "Development and Learning." *Journal of Research in Science Teaching* 2(3): pp.176-186, 1964.

16. For a complete discussion of the four factors, see John Renner and Edmund Marek, *The Learning Cycle* (Portsmouth, New Hampshire: Heinemann, 1988).

10. Ibid., p. 41.

18. John Renner, Michael Abraham, and Howard Birnie, "The Occurrence of Assimilation and Accommodation in Learning High School Physics." *Journal of Research in Science Teaching* 23(7), 1986.

19. Francis and Edith Schaeffer, *Everybody Can Know* (Wheaton, Illinois: Tyndale House Publishers, 1973), p. 153

20. C.S. Lewis, *The Silver Chair* (New York: Macmillan Publishing Co., Inc., 1970), pp. 122-125.

21. Ibid., pp. 150-157.

RESOLVE NUMBER FOUR

1. As quoted by Bill Bright, *The Holy Spirit: The Key to Supernatural Living* (San Bernardino, California: Here's Life Publishers, 1980), p. 4.

2. Watchman Nee, *Christ: The Sum of All Spiritual Things* (New York: Christian Fellowship Publishers, Inc., 1973), pp. 13, 19.

3. Francis Schaeffer, *Two Contents, Two Realities* from *The Complete Works of Francis Schaeffer: A Christian Worldview* (Wheaton, Illinois: Crossway Books, 1982), Vol. 3, p. 416.

4. V. Raymond Edman, *They Found the Secret: Twenty Transformed Lives that Reveal a Touch of Eternity* (Grand Rapids, Michigan: Zondervan Publishing House, 1984), pp. 3-4.

5. Ibid., pp. 135-137.

6. Francis Schaeffer, *True Spirituality* from *The Complete Works of Francis Schaeffer: A Christian Worldview* (Wheaton, Illinois: Crossway Books, 1982), Vol. 3, p. 237.

7. Jean Sibelius, "Finlandia."

8. Katharina von Schlegel, "Be Still My Soul."

9. Andrew Murray, *Absolute Surrender* (Westwood, New Jersey: Barbour and Company, 1984), pp. 172-188.

10. V. Raymond Edman, *They Found the Secret: Twenty Transformed Lives that Reveal a Touch of Eternity* (Grand Rapids, Michigan: Zondervan Publishing House, 1984), pp. 3-4.

11. As quoted by Bill Bright, *The Uniqueness of Jesus* from *Ten Basic Steps Toward Christian Maturity* (Orlando, Florida: Campus Crusade for Christ, 1983), p. 17.

12. Ernest Hemingway, *The Old Man and The Sea* (New York: Macmillan Publishing Company, 1980).

13. As quoted by Bill Bright, *The Uniqueness of Jesus* from *Introduction: Ten Basic Steps Toward Christian Maturity* (Orlando, Florida: Campus Crusade for Christ, 1983), p. 17.

RESOLVE NUMBER FIVE

1. Brent Lamb, and John Rosasco, *Household of Faith* (The Sparrow Corporation, 1986).

2. "When You Wish Upon A Star", *Pinocchio*, 1940.

3. Edith Schaeffer, *What Is A Family* (Old Tappan, New Jersey: Fleming H. Revell Company, 1975), p. 119 - 147.

4. Oswald Chambers, *My Utmost for His Highest: September 12th* (New York: Dodd, Mead, and Company, 1935), p. 256.

RESOLVE NUMBER SIX

1. Francis Schaeffer, *Back to Freedom and Dignity* from *The Complete Works of Francis Schaeffer: A Christian Worldview* (Wheaton, Illinois: Crossway Books, 1982), Vol. 1, p. 357-358.

2. Gladys Hunt, *Honey for a Child's Heart* (Grand Rapids, Michigan: Zondervan Publishing House, 1978) , p. 11.

3. Ibid., p. 26.

4. John Lennon and Paul McCartney, *Meet the Beatles!* (Los Angeles, California: Capital Records).

5. Jane Stuart Smith and Betty Carlson, *The Gift of Music* (Wheaton, Illinois: Crossway Books, 1995), p. xii.

6. Ross Campbell, *How To Really Love Your Child* (Wheaton, Illinois: Victor Books, 1978), pp. 55-66.

7. Edith Schaeffer, *Lifelines* (Wheaton, Illinois: Crossway Books, 1982), p. 13.

8. Harry Chapin, "Cat's in the Cradle" (Electra, Warner Communications Company, 1974).

RESOLVE NUMBER SEVEN

1. *What in the World is Real: Challenging the Superficial in Today's World* (Champaign, Illinois: Communication Institute, 1982), p. back cover.

2. John W. Whitehead, *The Second American Revolution* (Wheaton, Illinois: Crossway Books, 1988), p. 169.

3. Ibid.

4. Jerram Barrs, *What in the World is Real?* (Champaign, Illinois: Communication Institute, 1982), p. 47.

5. Jackson Pollock, Number 1, (Lavender Mist), National Gallery, 1950.

6. John Walker, *National Gallery of Art* (New York: Abrams, 1995), p. 614.

7. Francis Schaeffer, *How Should We Then Live?* from *The Complete Works of Francis Schaeffer: A Christian Worldview* (Wheaton, Illinois: Crossway Books, 1982), Vol. 1, pp. 200-201.

8. Percy Scholes, *The Concise Oxford Dictionary of Music* (London: Oxford University Press, 1964), p. 254.

9. Edward Gibbon, *Decline and Fall of the Roman Empire* (New York: Dutton, 1910).

10. Percy Scholes, *The Concise Oxford Dictionary of Music* (London: Oxford University Press, 1964), p. 254.

11. Donald Grout, *A History of Western Music* (New York: Norton and Company, 1973), pp. 726-727.

12. Ibid., p. 706.

13. Jane Stuart Smith and Betty Carlson, *The Gift of Music* (Wheaton, Illinois: Crossway Books, 1995), p. 65.

14. Robert McCloskey, *Blueberries for Sal* (New York: The Viking Press, 1948).

15. Gene Stratton-Porter, *Let Us Highly Resolve* (London: Hutchinson and Co., Ltd.), pp. 287-288.

16. John Eidsmoe, *Christianity and the Constitution* (Grand Rapids, Michigan: Mott Media Book, 1987), p 51.

17. Ibid., p. 21.

18. "Beyond the Year 2000: What to Expect in the New Millennium." *Time*, 1992.

19. *The Giants of Philosophy: Plato* (Nashville, Tennessee: Knowledge Products, 1990).

20. C.S. Lewis, *The Silver Chair* (New York: Macmillan Publishing Co., Inc., 1970), p. 157.

POSTSCRIPT

1. Gene Stratton-Porter, *Let Us Highly Resolve* (London: Hutchinson and Co., Ltd.), p. 261.

2. Ibid., pp. 278-279.

David and Shirley are committed to equipping parents disciple their children based upon the Biblical world view. If you want more information or would like to secure David and Shirley for a speaking engagement, you may contact them through their organization:

The Cornerstone Curriculum Project
www.cornerstonecurriculum.com
2006 Flat Creek Place
Richardson, Texas 75080
972-235-5149

—————————— ❦ ——————————

Educational materials for discipling your children to reason from the Biblical world view written and produced by David Quine include:

- *Making Math Meaningful*
- *Principles from Patterns — Algebra I*
- *Science: The Search*
- *Music & Moments with the Masters*
- *Classical Composers and the Christian World View*
- *Adventures in Art*
- *World Views of the Western World: A Classical High School Education*

—————————— ❦ ——————————